INTIMATE STRANGERS

INTIMATE STRANGERS

Men and Women Together

LILLIAN B. RUBIN

HARPER & ROW, PUBLISHERS, New York

Cambridge, Philadelphia, San Francisco,
London, Mexico City, São Paulo, Sydney

1817

The case histories and examples in this book are based on actual situations, but in some instances the cases described are composites of several actual cases and in all instances the name and all indentifying details about each person have been changed. Thus, the situations described are fairly represented, but are not actual or descriptive of any individual.

FIRST EDITION

Designed by Ruth Bornschlegel

Library of Congress Cataloging in Publication Data

Rubin, Lillian B.
  Intimate strangers.

  Includes index.
  1. Women—Psychology. 2. Men—Psychology. 3. Interpersonal relations.
4. Intimacy (Psychology). 5. Sex role. I. Title.
HQ1206.R77 1983   305.3   82-48678
ISBN 0-06-014922-1

83 84 85 86 87 10 9 8 7 6 5 4 3 2 1

FOR HANK
With my deepest gratitude—
for what he is and what we share

Contents

Acknowledgments   ix

(1) The Changing Dream   1

(2) New Roles, New Rules   16

(3) The Child Within   38

(4) The Approach-Avoidance Dance:
    Men, Women, and Intimacy   65

(5) The Sexual Dilemma   98

(6) Redefining Dependency   120

(7) Love, Work, and Identity   160

(8) Raising the Children Together   184

(9) People in Process   205

Index   217

Acknowledgments

First and foremost, my gratitude goes to the people who allowed me to enter their lives—who shared their hopes, their dreams, their joys, and their disappointments in their own intimate relationships. Without them, this book wouldn't have been possible. Therefore, it's to them that I owe a special debt—a debt that can only be repaid by honoring not just the content of their life stories, but the spirit of their lives as well. More than anything else, I have tried to do just that.

I am fortunate, indeed, to live in a community where there are more bright, spirited, creative minds in a square block than one has any right to expect. And more fortunate still that many of those wonderful minds and hearts have been available to help make this a better book. For the hours of discussion and for their thoughtful reading of all or part of this work my thanks to: Karen Axelsson, Ani Chamichian, Diane Ehrensaft, Peter Finkelstein, Susan Griffin, Arlie Hochschild, Dorothy Jones, Terry Kupers, Joyce Lipkis, Jim Lucas, Nancy Ringler, Kurt Schlesinger, Arlene Skolnick, Jerry Skolnick, Gladys Topkis, Barbara Waterman.

Edward Burlingame, my editor at Harper & Row, undertook that role at a difficult moment in the writing of this book. His sensitivity and his ability to grasp the meaning of the work I was trying to do even when it was not yet wholly formed have been invaluable. And Sallie Coolidge, who worked with me on the final version, made that part of the work very much easier by the sympathetic intelligence and humor she brought to it.

My agent, Rhoda Weyr, has, as always, been a wonderful friend and a provocative critic. She will, no doubt, recognize her mark on these pages.

Susan Romer Kaplan helped with some of the interviews early in the project—a task she undertook and completed with her usual intelligence and competence.

To Elaine Draper, my research assistant for the past five years, I owe a very special thanks. Throughout all these years and across several projects, she has done whatever work I set before her—even those jobs I knew she hated—quickly, quietly, intelligently, and without complaint. All of my work would have been harder without her; all of it is better because of her.

My patients deserve mention here, too, for they are a continuing source of learning and inspiration. In particular, the men and women of the Monday-afternoon group—who work so hard and so well—have helped me to understand and clarify many of the issues that arose in my research and writing. And, of course, those who have allowed me to use the material of their lives on the pages of this book have my deepest gratitude.

The research on friendship, which is discussed relatively briefly here, was supported by a three-year grant from the Behavioral Sciences Research Branch of the National Institute of Mental Health (MH 33624).

There are a few others who deserve special mention— friends and family, all important to my life in their own way, all who have been closely involved in the creation of this book.

Barbara Artson has, for many years now, been the sister I always yearned for but never had. Her grace, her intelligence, her humor, and, most of all, her capacity for a deeply intimate relationship have been a gift for which there is no recompense.

Kim Chernin's prodigious intellect and superb editorial abilities have made their mark on every facet of this work. She has a special capacity to inspire me to rise to the very best that's in me, whether intellectual or emotional, for which I am always grateful.

Michael Rogin served on my dissertation committee many years ago when he was a young professor at Berkeley and I was finishing my graduate studies. At the time, I was astonished by his capacity to get into the work and mind of another person and offer a response from the inside rather than the outside. I envied that ability then; I still do. All of my work has benefited from our continuing relationship—this one perhaps more than most.

My daughter, Marcy, is always available to read, to talk, to commiserate when I'm down, to share the joy when I'm up. Yet, when I'm writing, she remains discreetly at a distance, hoping to protect me from still another intrusion on my time or my emotional energy. She is all that any mother could ask —my child and my intellectual and emotional peer.

Finally, there is my husband, Hank. Throughout the difficult months of writing and revising, he not only cooked every meal but read every word I wrote—more than once. We talked endlessly about the issues the book was raising, not just in some abstract discussion, but about our own lives and what we could come to understand through the work I was doing. We both changed and grew in the process; our relationship deepened even after twenty years of living together; and we came away with more hope for intimate relations between women and men than we had before I started. In some important ways, this book is as much his as it is mine. That is why I have dedicated it to him.

Lillian Rubin

El Cerrito, California
October 1, 1982

INTIMATE STRANGERS

(1)

The Changing Dream

"I LOVE YOU"—MAGICAL WORDS, longed for, hoped for, dreamed about. "I love you"—words that hold out the promise that loneliness will be stilled, that life will at last be complete. Once, not so long ago, we heard those words and thought about forever. Once, they signaled the end of the search, meant that we would marry and live happily ever after. Now, we're not so sure.

Who really knows how "happy" ever-after was? What we do know is that the dream of that earlier time seemed a simpler one. Women and men each had a place—a clearly defined, highly specific set of roles and responsibilities that each would fulfill. She'd take care of home and hearth; he'd provide it. She'd raise the children; he'd support them. She'd subordinate her life to his, and wouldn't even notice it; her needs for achievement and mastery would be met vicariously through his accomplishments or those of the children.

It seemed fair then—a tidy division of labor not often questioned. It was, after all, in the nature of things, in the nature of women and men—what they expected of themselves, what they expected of each other. Now, we're not so sure.

As time tested it, as the world changed, it became clear that the old dream didn't work so well for most people most of the time. Marriages staggered under the burden of these role definitions; the dream began to look like a nightmare. Most women couldn't simply give themselves and their needs away so readily, at least not without some covert rebellion—rebellion that took the form of depression, of overcontrolling and demanding behavior, of nagging, or of any of the other ways in which women have sought to reclaim some parts of themselves and some power in their relationships with their men.

The men faced an equally difficult set of tasks. The tough, fearless, unemotional hero of folklore was a hard act to keep up in real life, the attempt carrying with it enormous emotional stress. In an economy that is almost always short on jobs, and in which most men who are lucky enough to have one simply can't earn enough to meet the idealized notions of male responsibility, making it in the world of work is no less problematic—especially when a man's accomplishments are supposed to do for two, when his successes are expected to serve for hers also. The disappointment of his own dreams would be hard enough to bear, but it hurts even worse when a man must face the knowledge that he has dashed hers as well.

More and more we have come to see that we made a bad bargain, if not an impossible one. More and more we have come to recognize that both men and women have been feeling helpless and angry—feelings that get acted out against each other all too often. Like hers, his rebellions, too, have come under the cover of behaviors not easily recognized as rebellious: hostile withdrawals; critical, perfectionist demands of wife and children; escapes into work, television, drinking, sometimes even violence.

But cultural ideals are powerful forces, shaping not only our ways of thinking and doing but our ways of being as well, giving form to both the conscious and unconscious content of our inner lives. Change, therefore, comes slowly, meeting enormous resistance both inside us and in the system of social institutions that supports our society's mandates about femininity and masculinity—about how a good woman lives, how a good man behaves.

Still, however haltingly, however incompletely, change does come. The ideal visions of one age eventually are seen as its excesses by the next. Thus, for example, the corseted repression that constrained the Victorian era was the yoke against which the succeeding generation strained. And the taut bonds of togetherness that were the mark of the 1950s became the target of rebellion by the youth of the 1960s. It was not just an obscene war, not just some abstraction called "society" that came under attack, but the very structure of the family itself and the relationships inside it. Togetherness was out; foreverness was called into question; commitment to another was edged aside by the search for self. Talk about the generation gap became part of our public dialogue and private agony as parents and children were separated by a shifting value system that opened up a huge chasm between them.

But change generally outruns consciousness, and, for most of us, change in consciousness lags well behind the changing social norms, sometimes even behind changing personal behaviors. Indeed, always, no matter how revolutionary a period of change may seem on the surface, the old myths continue to whisper to us. Consciously derogated, unconsciously avoided and denied, they continue to speak with a power and persistence that will not be dismissed. Consequently, two contradictory systems of ideals lie within us— the emerging one vying for dominance with the old one, new behaviors creating internal conflicts as they rub against obsolete but still living rules. Thus, even the children who initiated the change haven't wholly given up the happily-ever-after dream. They have instead made it time-limited. Each new relationship raises again the fantasy of eternal love and endless joy—the difference being that, when disappointment sets in, they feel freer now to move on to continue the search.

No small change, it's true. And the divorce and remarriage rates give testimony to the depth and breadth of the shift. But it isn't, as some critics have charged, simply selfishness, immaturity, narcissism, or some other newly discovered and widespread character flaw that makes binding commitments so difficult in the present era. To write such major social changes off with an analysis that focuses on personal psychopathology is to trivialize the impact of the social world on the lives of the people who live in it and to elevate psychology to a cause of our social malaise rather than an effect of it. For as Russell Jacoby puts it so pithily, "The social does not 'influence' the private; it dwells within it."*

In fact, the recent changes in family life are related to a complicated set of social forces, not least of them the coming together of changes in the economy with important demographic shifts in the society. The burgeoning number of women in the work force, for example—which is surely a central, if not always conscious, contributor to the shifting relations inside the family—is itself related both to economic factors and social ones. The increasing emphasis on consumer goods and the continuing inflationary spiral are two good reasons why so many women have flocked into the labor force over the last two decades. But without the medical advances that have dramatically increased longevity, and without the development of modern birth-control methods which make it possible to regulate with some certainty the number and spacing of children, such a shift would not have been possible. All together, however, such changes in

Social Amnesia (Boston: Beacon Press, 1975), p. 104.

the world outside the family have profound effects on what happens inside it. That, in turn, affects the family's relationship to both the society and the economy. And, ultimately, all these changes interact to set in motion transformations in the whole meaning and vision of masculinity, femininity, marriage, and adulthood.

This is the situation we find ourselves in today. Advances in health and medical technology have brought striking advances in longevity.* From 1920 to 1978, the life expectancy for women jumped almost twenty-three years, from 54.6 to 77.2. For men, the rise is somewhat less dramatic but still impressive: from 53.6 years to 69.5. Not many years ago, fertility control was a matter of chance and a product of luck. The Pill and the IUD changed all that. And the birth rate dropped from 24.1 per thousand population in 1950 to 15.3 in 1978, while the average number of children per woman fell sharply—from 3.5 in 1950 to 1.9 in 1980.

The increase in longevity means that, for the first time in our history, if we marry at twenty-five, we will have before us, on the average, forty-five years to live together. The decline in the birth rate means that, also for the first time, a substantial portion of those years will be free of childrearing responsibilities.

Such facts have important consequences for the conduct of both marriage and adulthood. They color how we think about our lives, how we plan to live them, what we come to expect in our interactions with each other. Indeed, it is out of such changes that we might say that adulthood has been "discovered" in this age in the same way that childhood was the discovery of the seventeenth century† and adolescence of

---

*The statistics that follow are taken from United States Bureau of the Census, *Statistical Abstract of the United States: 1981* (102nd edition). Washington, D.C., 1981.

†Philippe Ariès, *Centuries of Childhood: A Social History of Family Life* (New York: Vintage Books, 1972).

the late nineteenth.* Adolescence as a distinct stage of life became possible when the transformation in production wrought by the Industrial Revolution was complete and children no longer were needed in the factories. And adulthood, as we conceive it today, becomes possible as we have fewer children, live longer, and shift from a production to a service economy in this post-industrial age.

Philippe Ariès, the French historian who documented the discovery of childhood so brilliantly, noted, for example, that in sixteenth-century France there was no concept of a stage in life between youth and old age.† Youth was the prime time; after that came old age and death. It seems strange to us now, but, in an era when forty was very old, it made sense. Today, when forty is still young, adulthood becomes a stage of life that brings with it extraordinary new possibilities for living—and a whole new set of problems. Personal change, growth, development, identity formation— these tasks that once were thought to belong to childhood and adolescence alone now are recognized as part of adult life as well. Gone is the belief that adulthood is, or ought to be, a time of internal peace and comfort, that growing pains belong only to the young; gone the belief that there are marker events—a job, a mate, a child—through which we will pass into a life of relative ease.

Thus, just as marriage is not necessarily an enduring commitment anymore, adulthood is no longer an event, something we achieve at a given moment in our lives—when we reach a certain age, when we pass through a particular stage, when we assume what have, in other times, been called "adult responsibilities." Even the language we use

---

*David Bakan, "Adolescence in America: From Idea to Social Fact," in Jerome Kagan and Robert Coles, eds., *From Twelve to Sixteen: Early Adolescence* (New York: W. W. Norton, 1972).

†Ariès, *op. cit.,* p. 25.

tells the difference. For we don't speak, as we used to, of *stepping into adulthood,* we talk instead of *becoming adult* —the one connoting a crossing of a line, a static achievement; the other implying a dynamic process that includes change, growth, and development as continuing aspects of adult life.

But there's uncertainty abroad—a trembling uncertainty that makes us anxious, fearful, ill-at-ease. If falling in love gives no guarantee of eternal happiness, what will? If peace, quiet, and contentment are not the rewards of adult life, what can we look for? If dependability, commitment, conformity, and sacrifice are out, what's in? If change, not stability, becomes the watchword of these years, how do we come to know and to define ourselves; how do we learn to live with ourselves, let alone with each other?

These are difficult questions and trying times; contradictions plague us wherever we turn. At one level, for example, we talk about happiness, often look as though we're in a frantic search for it. At another level, "struggle" is the injunction most commonly heard these days. Happiness, in this context, is seen as some kind of mindless stagnation rather than a valued prize. No pain, no gain, we're told. Living is hard, whether alone or together; relationships don't just happen; love is not something we find or fall into. It all requires work—hard work—without guarantee of reward, often without even understanding what the reward might be.

Interesting ideas, aren't they, for what has been called a narcissistic and hedonistic age? And puzzling, too, because intuitively we think: Both are true. We *have* refused to accept the old definitions of adult life, the old ways of relating to each other. Even those of us who don't believe our sole responsibility is to "look out for number one" now insist upon our right not to relinquish self to the interest of others. But our Puritan heritage and frontier mentality still haunt us. And our personal quest is culturally acceptable only in the context of painful struggle—the heroic conquest of yet another frontier, only this time not a geographic one. Perhaps never in history have we expected so much and so little at the same time; never before have we seen such an odd conjunction of heightened expectations about the possibilities in human relationships and disillusion, if not despair.

It is precisely this paradox that gives this era its unique and provocative flavor. Indeed, this is the paradox that has eluded some of our most distinguished social commentators, and that accounts for the common experience among us of reading or hearing an analysis of the ills of present-day society that leaves us with the uncomfortable sense that it is both right and wrong at the same time. It's not our perceptions that are off, but an analysis that has failed to come to grips with these contradictory impulses which, from one view, make this look like the age of hedonism and, from another, give it a distinctly ascetic stamp.

The new dream, then, is not a simple one, often not even coherent and clearly understood by most of us who are trying to live it. We know that the old ways are not for us, but have no clear picture yet of what the new ones will be. We know there's a new vision of masculinity and femininity, but can't figure out how it fits each of us. Men ask themselves: If we're no longer supposed to be the strong, silent, masterful ones, what are we to be; how are we to act? And women want to know: If femininity is no longer to be defined by passivity, helplessness, cuteness, and coyness, what will take their place? If masochism is out of fashion, what's in?

We talk about equality between women and men, then ask ourselves: What does it mean? We say we want intimacy, companionship, sharing, but don't always know just what we're looking for. We tell each other we must communicate better, but often have no idea where or how to start the process. We're told that one problem is our inability to express anger, so we read books and take lessons in how to do it, but none of it seems to work. We go to therapists to work on our relationships, but can't say what we really want from each other.

This is the struggle in which women and men are engaged today, both with each other and within themselves. We talk about our relationships, think about them, worry about them, ask ourselves why it is that they seem so difficult. Yet we have no answers that make sense to us. *Intimacy, companionship, sharing, communication, equality*—these are the qualities of relationships we value most highly, we say. We work for them, struggle for them, analyze ourselves and our loved ones, seemingly without end. Still they elude us. We tell ourselves it's the way we were raised, that we will do better with our children. Then we stand back in pained and weary amazement as we watch our little boys behave in typical "boy" fashion, and our little girls behave in characteristic "girl" style. "So young," we say to ourselves despairingly, "how does it happen so young?" "Maybe we have been wrong," we think silently, even guiltily, not daring to say the words aloud. "Could it really be that these qualities we call 'masculine' and 'feminine' are built into the genes?"

Could it? For over a decade now, feminist scholars of both genders have labored to put before us a new vision of the nature of men and women and of the sources of the differences between us. At one level, the words persuade us; at another, the old questions bedevil us with haunting persistence. We argue with ourselves and with each other, unable to understand why what we believe doesn't always match what we see; why, despite our best efforts at nonsexist child-rearing, our daughters are still preoccupied with dolls, our sons with trucks. And we ask ourselves quietly, "Could it really be . . . ?"

Our own experiences add to the confusion. For even when we're quite clear about the direction of the change we're aiming for—even when men know they want more contact with what we call the "feminine" side and women look for stronger connections to their "masculine" half—getting there can be so fraught with conflict that we begin to wonder, "Could it really be . . . ?"

Over the last fifteen years, I have watched as women and men (my husband and I among them) struggle to change, noting with wonder the intransigence with which old ways hang on even when good intentions oppose them vigorously. As a social scientist, I have studied many hundreds of relationships intensively—examining the kinds of conflicts that preoccupy couples in our time, looking at how the issues that divide them are made manifest, how they are resolved. As a psychotherapist, I have worked with a very large number of women and men, singly and in couples, as they try to deal with the conflicts their attempts to change stir within and between them. As a woman, I have lived in a relationship with a man for most of my adult life—experiencing my fair share of the pain and pleasure to be found there, struggling to reduce the dissonance when the changing vision is at odds with inner experience. And always the questions loom: Why? Why is it so hard? Does it have to be this way?

If these years of watching and listening, of asking and answering, of reading and writing, of living and struggling have taught me anything about family life and the way we live it today, it is this: There is no single truth to tell. Looked at one way, it would be easy to say that life goes on much the same inside families. Turn the prism, and dramatic changes come into view. Thus, the one truth we can count on in relations between men and women today is that things are both the same and changing all the time—so much so that people often are confused themselves about what in their lives together is the same, what is different.

Of one thing I am convinced: The social world in which we live is the breeding ground for our internal psychological states. As we move toward new ways of being, we come up against social constraints that give way only very slowly. If and when we finally succeed in pushing past them, we meet psychological barriers that must be overcome. Therefore, to think about mass psychological changes without fundamental changes in the social institutions within which we live and grow is to give in to fantasy. Of those institutions, none influences the experience of adult life more profoundly than the family. For it is there that the very structure of male and female personality is formed—not by accident, not by biology, but by the nature of the traditional roles and relationships that have, until now, existed unquestioned there. But, once that psychology is rooted inside us, it develops a reality of its own. And it is an equally impossible dream to think that psychological change will follow immediately on the heels of social change.

Yet this is the contest that engages us so intensely today —a contest in which so many of us are struggling to rescue at least some part of self from society. It excites us, drains us, and bewilders us as we waver between triumph and despair—telling of our victories one moment, of our defeats the next.

It's just this shifting and changing reality—both in the external world and in our inner one—that makes a book about relations between men and women so difficult an undertaking. For writing is a logical and linear enterprise while living is an interactive and dialectical one—a continuous process of action and reaction within which we are constantly, if not always consciously, contending with our contradictory needs for change and stability. We learn, grow, change, and cling to the past all at the same time—one of life's predicaments that can be at once frustrating and exciting and which none of us escapes, not even a writer who has taken upon herself the task of illuminating both change and stability in a historical moment when those forces are in a heady contention.

I am concerned here not just to spotlight the present realities, however, but to explain them as well.The central task I have set for myself is to show how certain characteristics of male and female personality come into being, why they persist, and how they affect the most basic issues of our relations with each other—from the way we play out our social roles to the deep-seated internal differences between us on such issues as dependency, intimacy, sexuality, work, and parenting.

I depart from traditional socialization theorists in that I believe we must look beyond learning theories or theories of role modeling to understand the pervasiveness and persistence of these characteristic differences between us. And I depart from classical psychological theory in that I do not see a single line in child development—with one, the male, being defined as normal and the other, the female, characterized as a deviation from that norm. Instead, I will insist that while certain developmental imperatives exist for children of both genders—for example, the establishment of a continuing and coherent sense of self and gender identity—the tasks that confront a girl and a boy are quite different, resulting in different patterns of personality for each of them. These are the differences which, on the one hand, are at least partly responsible for the attraction between men and women and, on the other, create so many of the problems that exist between us.

But I will insist also that those different tasks, and the psychological differences that stem from them, are not inherent in the nature of human development, but are a response to the social situation—in particular to the structure of roles and relationships inside the family—into which girls and boys are born and will grow. From birth onward psyche and society engage in a complex and dynamic interaction. Our earliest experiences in the family lay the basis for our characteristic ways of being, and the cultural command-

ments about masculinity and femininity reinforce and solid-
ify them.

A question arises here: Are there no differences across
class, race, ethnic groups? The answer: Of course there are.
Whether a family is rich or poor, sick or well, black or white;
where they live and how; what work they do—all these are
crucial to understanding what issues of living become problems for them and how those problems are attended to. Thus,
for example, in a family where a mate is seriously ill, the
quality of intimacy in the relationship may not, for the moment, be a central concern. Similarly, if children are hungry,
a husband and wife are likely to be more concerned about
how to find food than whether they can talk about it.

Even when survival issues are not at stake, class makes
a difference in how people live, what they value, what they
wish for themselves and for their children—all of which I
have written about at length elsewhere.* In that earlier
work, I was interested in examining these differences with
a view to understanding the experiences of working-class
life that lead to the development of a class culture—ways of
being and living that enable people to cope and to survive.
And while such differences are not to be dismissed as irrelevant or unimportant in understanding life in these United
States, neither are the similarities that exist across all the
boundaries of group and class—similarities born of being
part of the same society, living in the same historical moment, facing the universal issues of family life: work, lei-
sure, childrearing, interpersonal relations. It's certainly true
that class, race, and ethnic differences give a special cast to
the shared experience. But that only means that there will be
variations among the groups—some which may be culturally
unique, others which may simply be subcultural variations

*Lillian Breslow Rubin, *Worlds of Pain: Life in the Working-Class Fam-
ily* (New York: Basic Books/Harper Colophon, 1976).

on the themes of the dominant culture.

My argument, then, is that the large social changes of our times affect us all. The advances in medical technology which have given us more years to live are met with technological changes in the work world—whether in the factory, the office, or the home—which almost require that we find new ways to live them. Our class situation will define the ways in which we approach these changes, and, all too often, it will limit the solutions that are possible for us. But the effects of the changes themselves, and the new aspirations that come on the heels of them, are felt across class and ethnic groups.

In the research for this book, I didn't have to look far or probe deeply to find that the hunger for something different in our relationships is profound and widespread. It's there, all across the country, to be seen by anyone who would look —from the eagerness with which men and women from all walks of life are ready to talk of these issues, to the tens of thousands of couples who have attended the various marriage enrichment programs whose appeal across class and ethnic groups, in this country and abroad, has been both astonishing and revealing.

But the style with which we express our concerns—and even what we consider acceptable to express—will differ from one class to another. So a woman who grew up in a family with a father who was drunk, violent, and only intermittently employed tells me that she prizes her husband because "he's a steady worker; he doesn't drink; and he doesn't hit me." But that doesn't mean she doesn't yearn for companionship with him as well. She may remind herself that she's better off than her mother was, may reprove herself because she's not unambivalently grateful. But, with all that, there remains a part of her that feels cheated, as if something is missing. Just so, her husband may tell himself he should be content with a life in which he has a steady job, a wife who's constant, who takes good care of the house and children, who doesn't nag too much. But he's restless—feeling that some promise in life remains unfulfilled, looking for something without knowing what. And when such feelings surface, wife and husband turn to each other—wanting something else in this marriage but unable to say what it is, blaming each other but not really knowing why.

On the pages that follow I shall present the experiences of people living in committed relationships—usually legal marriages but sometimes not. The book itself is a distillation of fifteen years of research on marriage and the family, of as many years of work as a psychotherapist, and of interviews done especially for this project with 150 couples between the ages of twenty-five and fifty-five who have been together for at least five years, some for thirty-five, most somewhere in between—people from diverse sections of the country and from all walks of life.

The question that guided this work throughout was: Why is it that change comes with such difficulty? It's in pursuit of the answer that we look first at people who, in many ways, are in the vanguard of the struggle for change yet who have found that—even when determination is high, even when good intentions are beyond question—changing old ways of doing and being is hard indeed.

(2)

New Roles, New Rules

Seldom, or perhaps never, does a marriage develop into an individual relationship smoothly and without crises; there is no coming to consciousness without pain.

CARL GUSTAV JUNG

NEW ROLES, NEW RULES—men and women living together and trying to change. Once, we thought it would be easy, that we need only see what had to be done and we could do it. Now, we see some progress in our efforts to change, and we see also the regress—the resistances in both our external world and our internal one that stand in the way of consolidating the headway we make. Now, the answers no longer come so readily; instead, there are questions to haunt us: "Why does change come so slowly and with such difficulty? Does it have to be this way?"

A thirty-eight-year-old man and his thirty-six-year-old wife—he, an engineer; she, a graphic designer for the last four years—tell the story of a marriage, in many ways typical for its time, and the pressures to change it. The husband:

> I was twenty-one when we got married—just finished college. Beth wasn't twenty yet, I think. We just did what everybody did—no thoughts about it, just did it. I was tied up with my career march; that's what I was concentrated on. It never occurred to me I was missing anything, or that there was some other way to live—not until Beth began pushing me.

The wife:

> I didn't even know I was miserable in those early years. I'd
> look around me and see that some men were really demanding
> bastards, and I'd say to myself, "See how lucky you are; Ted's
> not like that." When I look back at it now, it seems as if I was
> totally mindless.

The husband:

> In retrospect we'd both say I had a firmer idea about what I
> wanted. A man gets planted on a path early in life and he just
> goes toward it.

The wife:

> You ask me what I expected when I got married, and I don't
> know that I can tell you—someone to take care of me maybe,
> and fun. I don't know, maybe what I expected was not to have
> to think about what I would do with my life.

The husband:

> Somebody (was it Freud?) said work and love are the major
> things in life. I guess she felt the things that were tied to love
> were much more her responsibility and she was shut out of
> the world of personal creation and work. And I was like a
> robot, shut out of knowing much about loving. But that's hind-
> sight; we didn't either of us know it then.

The wife:

> It worked for a while, but after the children were born, things
> seemed to fall apart. I would nag him to be home more and
> take more responsibility; there was a lot of bitterness and
> whining. Then sex got to be not so great. Lots of conflict and
> trouble. It was as if I suddenly knew this wasn't a whole life
> I was living. I'd always been a bright, talented kid, and it was
> all going to waste. I had to do something, but I needed Ted to
> help me.

The husband:

> Little by little it got through to me what was happening. I felt
> like I had a gun at my head because I knew this family

couldn't survive the way it was. We were heading for disaster like so many of our friends—all getting divorced—and I knew I didn't want that. Never!

The wife:

I went back to painting and designing seven years ago, but this time I took myself seriously. There was an atmosphere—an environment because of the women's movement, I guess—that made it possible. Maybe because I did, other people, including Ted, took me seriously, too. Four years ago I got my first real job as a designer, and it's been on the upswing ever since. I love what I'm doing; it's as if the world suddenly opened up for me. Ted's been forced into a new relationship with the kids because I'm not so available anymore, and I actually think he loves it. Ask him.

The husband:

I started out scared of what would happen to us, but it's been great. I've gotten to know my kids—really know them—and that may be the biggest gift of all. At first, Beth wasn't making enough money to make much difference. But now . . . what a relief! I never knew it felt like such a big load to support the family until I found out it wasn't all mine anymore. It's like when you know it's safe to feel something, you let it happen. Well, that's the way it was. All of a sudden I understood that a lot of the time when I was behaving like a damn *macho* bastard, I was just mad as hell at having to take care of them all. That's what happened to her, too. Only with her, the anger came out in being a whining, bitchy nag.

The wife:

Look, we still have problems. I don't want you to think I'm living in some crazy dream world where we go off hand in hand to live happily ever after. But there's something real about our life together now, and we're much closer than we were before because we have some real understanding about how the other half has lived, you might say. He knows a little bit more now about what it's like to be worried about the kids because they're your very own responsibility. It's still not as much as I'd wish for, but it's more than it was. And I'm learning plenty every day about the kind of stress you face in the world out there.

But—maybe you won't agree or maybe it's plain silly, I don't know—sometimes I think there are some basic differences between men and women that we'll never change. I mean, we do okay on some things, then on others it's practically nowheresville. Well, not quite, I guess, but it feels like that sometimes, and then I have to remind myself that it's so much better than before and I shouldn't complain. It makes you wonder, though, doesn't it?

The husband:

It's not perfect, but, what the hell, what is? We have our differences, and maybe we're stuck with them, I don't know. It seems that way sometimes. We can get to a certain place then [his words trailing off] . . . I don't know exactly how to put it, but things don't jell again. When that happens, it can get pretty discouraging and you begin to feel hopeless. I mean, we do all right now most of the time when it comes to sharing responsibilities around here. But there's other stuff that's still a problem. Beth still complains that I don't get with it like she does, and then I begin to wonder whether there's anything I can do that'll be enough. Then we'll have an argument and I'll say that, but she'll insist that's not the point. So what is? [With a short, ironic laugh] I'm an old song buff and there's a line from one of those oldies that keeps going around in my head: "It ain't what you do but the way that you do it." Maybe that's what it all boils down to.

As I listened to these two, I was struck again by the difficulties we face when we try to transform the dream into a reality. For here, in this couple, are two people whose commitment to their marriage is unequivocal even while they're also aware that it requires some new rules—two people who already have experienced some of the benefits of changing the old roles. Yet there remains between them all that "other stuff that's still a problem."

Thinking about these issues took me back some dozen years in my own life. I had been a professional woman for just a short while, having gone to school late, when my daughter was already a teenager. Like Beth, I loved what I was doing; like her, I felt as if the world had just opened up before me. I was teaching at the time—a professor in a graduate school of psychology. Each time I approached the campus, I marveled at this miracle that had befallen me, clasped it to myself to make certain it wouldn't vanish like a dream. I thought then, as I think now: "This must be what a young man feels at the first big break in his career." But I wasn't a young man, I was a middle-aged woman.

My husband, too, was middle-aged, as was his career. Although he had supported us without question or complaint for years, he had recently begun to speak about wanting to do something else with his life—perhaps to write. Teasingly, he would say, "You're the best investment I ever made," referring to the years of support while I was studying for my doctorate. More seriously, he commented one day, "You can't imagine what a relief it is to know you can support yourself." "Why didn't you ever say things like that before?" I asked. "I never knew it until now," he answered.

Surprised, I didn't quite know what to make of his words. "Men," I thought to myself somewhat irritably, "they never 'know'." But, even as impatience flared, I knew his words reflected an important truth—not just about him, not just about men, but about all of us.

I remembered my own first marriage—all those years when I didn't "know" either. Married at nineteen to an up-and-coming professional man, I spent years trying to fit myself to the model of the times: happy suburban housewife, charming hostess, helpmate to a husband's burgeoning career. I knew, of course, that I awoke most mornings wishing I could stay in bed. But I told myself I was just tired. I knew there was an uneasiness that lived inside me—nothing intense, nothing dramatic, just a low-level malaise. But I told myself I was just a chronic malcontent as I tried to brush it away. I knew I threw myself into activities outside my home with an energy that seemed frantic. But I told myself it was natural to behave that way about these important political matters that engaged me so deeply.

These thoughts and more came to remind me how easy it is to deny what we know, to rationalize away the knowledge that rises unbidden inside us when, for whatever reasons, it is felt as a threat. As I write these words, I'm reminded also of a man I met some years ago who told me of the poverty of his youth in the mountains of Kentucky—a bitter, grueling, isolated kind of poverty that's hard for an urban person to fathom. "We didn't even know we were poor; we just thought that was the way life was," he said, expecting me to understand. "You know," he went on when it was clear I did not, "people are only discontented if they have some vision of a different kind of life. Let me give you an example. When I was a kid, I had a runny ear as far back as I could remember. Then, when I was ten, a doctor came through the hills and gave me some medicine to clear up the infection. Until then, I took it for granted that everyone had a runny ear, and I didn't even notice that it hurt. Once I knew better, though, my expectations changed, and, the next time the infection came, I knew it was hurting, and I wanted somebody to do something about it."

It's true, of course, that we can only know those things that are in our experience, only make choices from the alternatives that exist in our consciousness. But, when it comes to how we live in relationships, there's another truth as well. For, all too often, we don't dare to know what we know; it's too dangerous to the only way of life we have known, to the life for which we have been prepared from infancy. So we do what we have to do—what our society tells us is fitting, depending on whether we're male or female.

This, then, is what my husband meant when he said, "I never knew." It came home to me even more sharply some time later. Our only child was preparing to graduate from college and planning her future. When she announced to us her decision to go to law school, I was flooded with an enormous sense of relief. "Good," I thought, "I can rest easier now that I know she'll be able to take care of herself after we're gone." Unbidden and unexpected as it was, the thought brought me to an internal standstill. I never knew! I knew I was concerned about her future, even worried about it sometimes. But, until that moment, I never knew that I didn't feel free to die until I could be reassured about how she would live. "My God," I said to myself as I recalled those earlier talks with my husband, "is this the burden he's carried all these years—not just for his child but for his wife as well?"

Two years and many discussions after the subject first was broached, we agreed that the time had come for him to change careers, to try to make his way as a writer. We knew he would earn little money for a while, maybe forever. But it didn't make any difference, we decided. I was, by then, very successful—doing research and writing, teaching, keeping up a private clinical practice—well able to support the family in the style to which we had all become accustomed. None of it would have been possible without the support he had given me. Now it was my turn—a turn I took willingly, even eagerly, I thought. But we were soon to be in for an unpleasant surprise.

After a month or two of exquisite, never-before-experienced relief, my husband fell into a six-month-long depression, and I into an equally long struggle with my anger. On the surface, nothing had changed in my own life. I went to the same places each day, saw the same people, did the same work. But underneath something had been altered profoundly.

Although I am not a child of privilege, having been brought up in a family where poverty was no stranger, until that moment I never knew what it meant to be responsible for the roof over my own head—let alone over the heads of my loved ones. That's what happens when you're born a girl rather than a boy. I had worked in my life, of course, but always as an auxiliary wage earner—first in my widowed mother's home, later in the family my husband and I made together, always in the illusion, at least, that it was voluntary. Now, for the first time, I was in the position that men know so well: If I didn't go to work today, there would be no money tomorrow. Now it was no longer voluntary but necessary to pay for the bread and the rent. And I hated it.

I was stunned at my own reaction. We had, after all, talked about it, planned it, decided in a mature, adult fashion that my income could well support the family; that he should be freed, finally, to do what he wanted. But speaking the words and living the results are two different things. Suddenly, we found ourselves face to face with our inner sense of the way things *ought* to be. Suddenly, we had to confront the realization that we were still dominated by the stereotypic images of male and female roles—images we would have sworn we had, by then, routed from our consciousness.

He struggled with his sense of failure, with the fear that somehow his very manhood had been damaged. I—the liberated, professional woman—was outraged and enraged that he wasn't taking care of me any longer. I felt as if he had violated some basic contract with which we had lived, as if he had failed in his most fundamental task in life—to keep me safe and cared for, to protect and support me.

I knew these feelings came from some very deep part of myself that had learned from earliest infancy to believe there would always be someone around, preferably a man, to ease my life. And I knew, also, that I didn't want such thoughts and the feelings they brought with them. I reasoned with myself, argued with myself, berated myself—all with no success. The sense of betrayal and the anger it brought with it plagued me—persistently, insistently, for many long months.

Suddenly, I wasn't sure whether I wanted to work anymore; it no longer seemed like such fun. It's one thing to work because you want to, another because you have to. It makes a difference, too, if working is defined as helping out—which is the way most married women characterize their presence in the work force—or as the mainstay of support for the family.

Parenthetically, it's the same difference that explains why men who help out around the house will so often say they can't understand why their wives complain so bitterly about their lives. They don't feel tyrannized by the repetitive tasks because they don't have to do them over and over again. They don't feel harassed by the responsibilities of household and child care because they aren't held accountable for them. So it is with women with working husbands. They're not bedeviled by worry about earning enough money because that's not their major obligation in the family. They don't experience the harshness of the work world with such intensity because they can tell themselves there's an out; they can leave.

It was only when the burden of supporting the family was dropped onto my shoulders that I could comprehend how oppressive a responsibility that is. It was then that I said to my husband, "I think you men are crazy to live your whole life this way. If I were a man, I wouldn't have waited for women to call for a liberation movement; I'd have led it." But such are the differences between men and women that he only looked at me gently, tenderly, and said, "No, if you were a man, you wouldn't have noticed it. Until women began to make their demands, it never occurred to me that I was oppressed. It just seemed as if I was doing what was natural—nothing more."

His depression passed, as did my anger, but not without

plenty of psychological work for both of us. Looking back, I'm still surprised at the intensity of the emotional response we each experienced. The rewards now are great; we're both doing just what we want and need. But so deep are the issues such a shift raises that, even all these years later, we still sometimes find ourselves thinking we ought to explain, still sometimes interpret defensively some comments from others, still periodically have some trouble squaring our beliefs, behavior, and feelings.

Partly we react thus because the social world generally is inhospitable to such major shifts in roles in the family. Even close friends still have trouble believing what they see. So they speak to us of their fears—wondering whether we are denying our own conflicts, worrying that we may be damaging our marriage. Such expressions of concern don't make it any easier, of course. But we have come to understand all too well that the source of the conflicts lies inside us, not outside—in our earliest experiences and understandings of what it means to be male and female in a society such as ours.

I used to wonder whether these problems were unique to us, born largely of the fact that we were responding to the situation from the consciousness of an older generation. "Perhaps," I would think, "it wouldn't happen that way with people in their thirties instead of their forties and fifties." But all the evidence of my recent research suggests that most adults—even those with the most enlightened modern consciousness—still have difficulty in accepting a role reversal of that magnitude. Smaller changes may be tolerated quite easily. But one that puts a woman in a position of economic superiority and a man in the dependent female role is quite another matter. Most men still can't cope with not being able to support the family, and most women still have difficulty in accepting the need to support themselves. A thirty-year-old staunch feminist whose principles have led her to abjure a legal marriage spoke about just this conflict with pain and puzzlement.

> I know it's only fair that we share in supporting our family, but it feels so lonely sometimes, and I have dreams about laying back and letting him do it. I even find myself getting angry that he won't do for me what my father did for my mother. It feels unfair, like I'm not getting something I deserve. I know it's not rational, but . . .

Most women also still have problems when they fear that their man isn't bigger, stronger, smarter, more accomplished than they are. Independence and the capacity to take care of oneself and others is still a prerequisite for manhood but not for womanhood—not just in a man's view but in a woman's as well, as these words from a rising young executive tell us so sharply.

> I feel terrible about it, but I know that if Roger can't get his act together our marriage is in jeopardy. It's not the money; I can support us all well enough. But—and I know you'll think this is crazy or something given the way we've been living our lives and all the things I believe in about men and women being equal and all that—but . . . boy, this is hard to say; Christ . . . well, here goes. I just don't think I can respect him if he isn't capable of taking care of his own family, even if he doesn't have to because I can.

And most men still struggle with the same set of beliefs, even as those old ideas conflict with the newer ones about masculinity and femininity, as her husband's words show.

> There's no way a man can be self-respecting if he can't be independent and take care of his wife and kids. Maybe I don't want to *have* to do it like my father did, but it has to be a choice. I mean, I have to know I can, and I think Linda does, too. I don't think she'd admit it out loud because it's not what she wants to believe, but I think we both know it. It would be okay if she wasn't successful, but I don't think either of us will be comfortable for much longer if I don't make it in this new business. It's like my last shot to do it in a way. I mean, she has

to believe I have what it takes—and maybe not just to be successful either, but more than her.

Which brings us again up against the same question, even if in slightly altered form: Why can't a man be "self-respecting" unless he can "take care of his wife and kids"? And why can't a woman respect him unless he's acting in that traditional role? It's easy enough to point to the social definitions of man and woman, wife and husband, and say, "There, that's why"—as we have done now for this last decade or more. But the answer no longer satisfies. Instead we have questions that beg for understanding.

Repeatedly, in both my research and my clinical practice, young women and men speak of their contradictory and conflictful feelings around these issues. They know what they *should* feel, but the inner response doesn't always match the external mandates. Ideologically, they're committed to breaking down the stereotypes of what men ought to do, how women ought to behave. But their emotions contradict their intellect. They know that the new roles and new rules make sense; they value the struggle to make them the reality of their own lives, of their children's lives; they wouldn't give it up. But they know, also, that it's not without cost, not without conflict—both internal and external—that too often get transmuted into conflicts with each other. All of which leaves us with the question: Why, after so much struggle, does it still happen that way most of the time?

On the outside, social disapproval of those who defy convention makes itself felt in countless ways. Parents often are disappointed in what they see. A young professional woman, the mother of two children, complains:

> Even my parents aren't supportive of the way we live. My father is shocked that Paul is so involved in family matters at the cost of his professional status. My mother tries to under-

stand, but she worries about the kids, the marriage falling apart, and on and on. [Angrily] It really pisses me off, but it also makes me nervous about what we do.

Her husband adds:

Her father lets me know in a lot of subtle ways that he thinks I'm not successful enough. And my parents—well, they have a vision of what their attorney son should be like. [With a deep sigh] And I just don't match it. I'm not headed for a partnership in some fancy law firm. I have a good job in the legal department of my firm, but in law that's not where the big money and high prestige are. [Passing his hands over his eyes wearily] So they're disappointed, I guess. I can understand their feelings, but it hurts because they haven't got much understanding about why I did it this way. My father's a very successful man and my mother's the very successful wife of this very successful man. It's not a model Kathy and I had any wish to emulate.

Friends, neighbors, siblings, and assorted other family members will have their say as well, since those who try to live by the new rules often stir controversy and anxiety in the people around them. Sometimes they're just seen as an interesting anomaly. More often they look to others like a model for the future and, depending on the values of the observer, will be seen either as a threat or a promise. One couple in their middle thirties, both police officers on the same force, talked about the difficulties they have encountered in both their personal and professional life. The husband, a sturdy, attractive man whose easy smile belies the tension that lives just below the surface calm with which he meets the world, says:

When Gail first decided she wanted to try out for the force, I got nothing but razzing from the guys. Most of them don't like women around; you know, they don't think they can do a man's job. It was hard there for a long time. I used to feel like I'd want to duck every time I walked into work, like there was somebody taking pot shots at me all the time. But I also figured she had a right. She was thirty-two or -three years old, something like that, the kids were growing up, and she had the idea that a woman should be doing something with her life—not like her mother who mostly just sits around waiting for time to pass.

"What made you able to understand her needs when other men around you were being so resistant?" I asked.

Jeez, I don't know if I can say that. We talked about it a lot. [With a short laugh] I mean, she talked, I listened. I guess we had some fights, too. But she's got a way of keeping the pressure on; I mean, she's a feisty one; she doesn't back down so easy. I don't know, after a while it only seemed fair. I figured after all, she'd raised the kids pretty much by herself and she did one hell of a good job, too. [With a long, thoughtful pause] And they were half grown already when she began to talk about all this stuff—about ten and twelve, I guess. I figured I owed her. She always stood by me and helped me out; it seemed right that I should support her.

You understand, at first I didn't know she wanted to be a cop; we would be just talking about her doing something but she wasn't saying what. When she said she wanted to become a police officer, that was something else. I mean, *the mother of my kids—a cop.* I thought she was nuts or something. And, you know, I worried about her, too. It's not the safest line of work these days. I remember thinking, Christ, this can't be happening to me; she doesn't really mean it. My first answer was "No wife of mine's gonna be a cop—no way, not on your life." But, like I said, once she makes up her mind, she holds on like a bulldog.

"How is it now that she's actually done it?" I asked.

Well, I guess it's okay most of the time. I still get some flak from some of the guys, but not as bad as before. She's been on the force for almost a year now and people can see that she doesn't ask for any special favors or anything like that because she's a woman. But when I hear her unit sent out on a call that could be dangerous, my stomach gets tied in a knot because I get scared, and I stay scared until I hear that pretty little voice of hers checking back in.

The wife, a pert woman, surprisingly small for the amount of energy she radiates, speaks of her experience:

> I'm excited about what I'm doing now and Wayne's getting used to it, too. I think he's really kind of proud of me now that he sees I can handle the job. And I did it without any special help from him, too. I made up my mind that I wouldn't be a drag on him, and I wouldn't all the time be asking for his help, and I haven't.

"How about things on the home front?" I asked. "Do you share responsibilities there, too?"

> Well, we don't always work the same shifts, and, when that happens, whoever's home takes care of the kids and their needs. I mean, there's not much real care they need anymore. But still, someone has to oversee things, or take one of them to the dentist, or to gymnastics, or whatever. Mostly I do all the cooking because Wayne's not worth much in the kitchen. We'd all starve if we had to depend on him for that. But he does his share of the housework now; I can't complain about that.

"You sound as if there's something you do want to complain about, though," I commented.

> Yeah, I sure do. The problem's not with us; we do pretty well at working things out, I think. It's with all the people around us—you know, the people we have to work with or our families and some of our friends. The men at work are better than they used to be, but I don't think they'll ever *really* accept a woman as an equal. And they give Wayne a hell of a hard time. He tries to tune them out, but, you know, these are guys he's worked with for ten years, and it's hard to have them riding you all the time. [With a sigh which turns quickly to anger] Damn! People just won't let you live your life if it's different from how they live theirs. It's like they feel threatened by how we're living now, so my sister is always finding some way to remind me that if I'm not careful I'll lose Wayne to some woman who will be glad to stay home and clean his house for him. Or my mother-in-law says she wouldn't tell anybody what I do because she's kind of ashamed of her son's wife doing such a thing, and blah, blah, blah. My mom's not so bad.

She tries to be more understanding, but she worries about us a lot—especially about the kids. And I think she's also afraid Wayne'll get tired of being married to a woman like me. She kind of reminds me that it's a woman's job to comfort a man —as if I'd forget.

When couples who are trying to reorder traditional arrangements in the family live in the large urban centers of the country, there's usually enough social support to take the worst sting out of the criticism they hear. For those who live in the smaller towns and cities across the nation, it's considerably more difficult to sustain the way of life they're trying to build. But, irrespective of where they live, along with the external pressures—and perhaps hanging on so persistently because of them—there are their own internal voices that remind them that they have not yet wholly abandoned the old values themselves. Thus, an attractive thirty-one-year-old mother of two who works full time tells of her guilt because she isn't living out the traditional script.

The thing that's hardest for me is living with my guilties because I'm not being that perfect little wife and mother like most of Phil's colleagues have—you know, doing the entertaining that'll help him get ahead, keeping things in perfect order around here so that he can attend to *his* career, all that stuff. You know what I mean; I don't have to spell it out.

Two weeks later, I listen to her husband speak of his anxiety because he's not doing his half as well as the men he knows who live by the old rules.

I know, I know, it's not supposed to be *only* my job to support the family anymore. But, when things get tight, both of us look to me to be the one to earn more money. And I'm the one who feels like I'm not cutting it, not her.

It's not just his male need to prove himself or her pervasive concern with family relationships that sets these feelings in motion. Both are there. And there, also, helping to keep those feelings alive, is the difference in earning power between women and men—a striking difference when we consider that women still earn less than sixty cents for every dollar earned by men.

In this family, they're both professionals. She's a teacher; he's a dentist. This means that his income potential probably is at least three times greater than hers. Consequently, he must bear the larger burden of shoring up the family economy in these inflationary times. That makes sense, we say to ourselves; it seems reasonable and just. And, if we accept the unstated assumptions underlying such differences in earning power, of course it does.

But what if we ask: What's sensible about the wage disparity between dentists and teachers? Don't they both do work that's socially valuable? Isn't it at least as important to educate our children as it is to fix their teeth? Put that way, we might well conclude that it's not so "reasonable and just" —that the disparity lies in the fact that one is dominantly women's work, the other, men's. And we might notice, too, that such differences permeate the entire wage structure of our economy—that we, as a society, have systematically devalued the work women do, thereby justifying this inequity.

The traditional argument for many of these wage discrepancies is that dentistry, for example, requires a longer training period than teaching, therefore should be better recompensed. But the reasoning doesn't hold up to scrutiny. College professors generally have as long a training period as doctors, longer than lawyers, dentists, or the captains of industry, yet generally earn nowhere near as much as any of these. The female clerk-typist in the office who is expected to have a high school diploma earns substantially less than the forklift operator in the warehouse where no one cares much about his educational background. And so on.

Even where men and women have the same schooling and hold the same credentials, women earn substantially

less than men do—a reality of life in the world of work that
holds true at all educational levels, from high school gradu-
ates to holders of advanced degrees. A United States Department of Labor study of earnings for 1981 found that women
were paid much less than men in virtually every occupation
where both were employed.* And it makes no difference if a
woman holds a high-prestige degree from an elite university
or if she's a graduate of some little-known local college; the
story is the same. For example, a recent survey of women and
men who received an MBA degree from Stanford University
in the mid-1970s shows that, by the time they had been in the
work force for four years, the men were averaging about
$35,000 a year, the women, $27,500.†

The researchers suggest that these salary discrepancies
are partly a product of the different attitudes and goals held
by men and women, with the men aiming much higher
than the women. And partly, they say, the differences are
due to the fact that it's a woman who leaves the work force
to care for young children or to follow a husband to a new
job. But these are not two separate phenomena; the one is a
direct outcome of the other. A woman who sets out to earn
an advanced degree in business administration already has
made a statement about her view of herself and her ambitions. But, because she's a woman, she will scale down her
aspirations to meet the requirements of marriage and parenting in ways that a man generally need not and will
not.

The economic realities of the last decade have, of course,
had a powerful impact on family life—both in what we do
and how we feel about it. Today, over half of all married

*See also Jay Cocks, "How Long Till Equality?" *Time,* Vol. 120 (July 12,
1982), pp. 20–29.
†Myra H. Strober. "The MBA: Same Passport to Success for Women and
Men?" In Phyllis Wallace, ed., *Women in the Workplace* (Boston: Auburn
House, 1981).

women are in the work force, compared to 30 percent a generation ago. The figures for married women with children under six years old are even more striking: almost 19 percent in 1960, close to 45 percent in 1980, twenty short years later.*
And, although in some of those families the fiction still is maintained that the woman doesn't have to work, many more than ever before acknowledge that the woman's earnings are necessary if the family is to maintain a way of life they all hold dear.

As recently as the early 1970s, when I was doing the research for a book on the lives of young working-class families, many of the men still said stoutly, "No wife of mine will ever work; she belongs at home with the kids."† Of course, many working-class women have always worked outside the home, and many of those I met then did also. But the men in those families felt it as a stigma, a public admission of their inadequacy, and often made their own and their wives' lives miserable over it. Similarly, the women often felt that a promise had been betrayed, that a husband's inability to support the family all by himself was some personal failure on his part. Perhaps both knew their responses were irrational, but they usually couldn't help feeling that way, couldn't control the behavior the feelings generated.

In those same families, and in others like them, it's a different story today. While still not wholly without conflict, husbands and wives more often openly acknowledge now that the women work because the family needs the money. It's easier to accept, of course, when almost everyone on the street, everyone in the extended family, faces the same predicament. One man, sighing nostalgically for the old days,

*United States Department of Labor, Bureau of Labor Statistics, "Employment in Perspective: Working Women," Report No. 653 (Washington, D.C.: United States Government Printing Office, 1981).
†Rubin, *op. cit.*

spoke for many when he said with a certain realistic resignation:

> Yeah, sometimes I wish it was like in the old days when a man was a man and a woman was a woman and there wasn't any mix-up about it. Everybody knew what their job was then, and they just did it like they were supposed to. Now, Christ, it's sure different, sure is. But it's never going to be like that again, no sir—not what with prices going up and up all the time. She'll be working for good, I guess, and I'm damn glad she can do it; we couldn't make it without what she brings in.

That new definition of the situation means that new rules are developing about the old roles. Just as a man feels freer to accept help from his wife outside the house, a woman is more able to expect help from her husband inside. It's true that quite often she'll still have a battle to get him to share in what has traditionally been defined as "woman's work." But perhaps equally often there's an elementary sense of fairness that comes into play. Minutes later, therefore, the same man adds:

> Maybe I don't do as much as I should, but I help out some—you know, with the kids and the housework. I even learned how to cook a little because she comes home later than me two days a week and everybody gets hungry. So I get the meal started those nights. It's only fair, isn't it? She helps out in her way, so I do in mine.

This is one of the places where class makes a difference. Among working-class families, tradition dies hard because life itself is harder, and it often feels as if survival depends on an adherence to ways that are known. Therefore, there's likely to be lots of talk about the value of the old while people actually live out important elements of the new. In the middle class, where choice—whether about work or lifestyle—is more readily possible, change itself is more highly valued. But this generally means only that the new roles and new rules tend to be given more credence in word than in deed.

In fact, in most families of any class, it's still defined as a husband helping his wife with her job and a wife helping a husband with his. Still, the boundaries of the jobs are considerably more blurred today than they were just a short time ago.

It may not seem like much in these times when expectations run so high, but ask yourself: How many men still have never changed a baby's diaper, never washed or dried a dish, never cooked an egg, never run a vacuum cleaner, never spent a day with the children while mother went off to work or play? How many men still are so divorced from the daily business of family life that they do not at least have some consciousness that it *ought* to be different? How many still believe unequivocally that a woman's place is inside the home, a man's place outside it?

But hardly do these words appear on the page before me when I begin to wonder, "What difference does it make what people believe; isn't it what they do that counts?" I reflect upon the question, turn it over and over in my mind, go back again to what I have seen and heard throughout my years as a student of family life in America. Finally I see that the question rests upon a view that's too simple, one that doesn't take account of the complex relationship between thought, belief, and behavior.

I know, of course, that beliefs are no guarantee of change, that behavior often lags well behind consciousness. But I know, also, that a changed consciousness is the forerunner of behavioral change—that without it change is all but impossible. And one of the things that's so interesting about trying to understand what goes on in the private regions of family life—what men and women actually do when the door is closed and they feel safe from the eyes of all observers —is that people both say more than they do and do more than they say. This means that sometimes, and about some things, they give lip service to the new ways while hanging on doggedly to the old. And, equally often, it's just the reverse. They speak in the language of traditional roles while moving inexorably toward the new ones.

New roles. They're hard to come by. Still we struggle toward them, working against social constraints and against those that live inside us. We argue about them, defend them, decry them in a debate that's noisy, often acrimonious. Yet all of us—including those who shout the loudest in defense of the old ways—have been touched by the new ones. Even that staunch opponent of the new feminism, Phyllis Schlafly, has gone to law school. Indeed, she has made an important career outside the home out of her opposition to the Equal Rights Amendment—not something her grandmother would have done so easily, even if she had been a suffragette.

But the years of struggle and conflict over new roles and new rules in the family have taught us that changing who works inside the house, who outside, and balancing those responsibilities more equitably is only one part of the problem—the one that, difficult though it may be, is more readily accessible to our direct interventions. The deeper issues lie in the struggle to change what happens *inside ourselves.* To see the depth at which the old ways live inside us, to grasp the power with which they influence adult life and behavior long after we have learned about new ways of being, and to understand fully the source of it all, we must go back to childhood.

(3)

The Child Within

The childhood shows the man,
As morning shows the day.
JOHN MILTON

THE LAST DECADE HAS SEEN a vast outpouring of social-science literature documenting the ways in which society and family come together to train girls and boys to their socially approved roles. From the first moment of life, the child is identified by its gender. "It's a girl!" "It's a boy!"—these exultant words are the first ones spoken in the presence of this newly birthed human being. And, from this moment forward, that identity is profoundly important in determining the shape of the human life to which it is attached.

Each society has a set of expectations about what is appropriate as feminine behavior, what acceptable as masculine. From birth onward those expectations are communicated to the child in numberless ways—ways that are sometimes so subtle as to defy easy observation either by the observer or the actor. A parent, for example, often is unconscious of the ways in which boys and girls are treated differently in the family, of the different messages the children get depending on their gender. In the earliest months of life, it just seems "natural" to handle an infant girl like a fragile china doll, a boy like the robust creature he is expected to be. Without thought, we look at a baby girl and say, "My, isn't she pretty," while an infant boy elicits such comments as, "Oh what a big, strong fellow he is." And, as they grow up and are able to share in the work of the family, it just seems "natural" that a girl will do the dishes and a boy will mow the lawn. Similarly, the framers of the textbooks children use in school don't consciously plan to subvert girls' initiative, playfulness, or aggressive qualities. It just seems "natural" to portray girls as the passive, nurturing supporters of the boys' activities. And, although the feminist ferment of recent years has brought many of these formerly unconscious behaviors into consciousness, others still remain unseen and not understood—still seem simply to reflect "natural" differences between girls and boys, men and women.

This is not to suggest that childhood determines adult life in some fixed and final form. Far from it. The capacity to learn, grow, change, even to transform ourselves, does not atrophy with adulthood. And, if the experiences of later life didn't reinforce those of our earliest years so effectively, change might come more easily to many of us. As it is, socialization to approved gender behaviors continues throughout our lives—the institutions of society quietly but artfully molding us into proper men and women in accordance with whatever are the accepted standards of the day, and making sure we stay that way.

Until recently I believed that we needed only to understand these forces for socialization to explain stereotypic gender behavior. But more than a decade of watching women and men struggle to change—often with only limited success—has convinced me that there are differences between us that are not *simply* a product of role learning and socialization practices. These are powerful and effective forces in shaping human life, of that there is no doubt. But we have, all of us, been living through a period of profound social change—an era when the old ideal standards of masculinity and femininity have come under severe attack. Yet even those of us who have been in the vanguard of the struggle for change often find ourselves in conflict between our new behaviors and our old consciousness. "Why?," I kept asking myself. "There must be something else necessary to explain the dogged persistence with which these ways of being resist our best efforts to change," I kept thinking. "Otherwise, why is it so difficult to unlearn our roles even when we have set our minds and hearts so firmly to the task?"

The answer, I now believe, lies in some deep-seated psychological differences between women and men—differences, I hasten to add, that are not born in nature but are themselves a product of the social organization of the family. To understand what this means to our lives, how profoundly it affects who we are and how we live, whether separately or together, let's go back to the beginning, to the day we are born.

Some life events are unique to each of us, of course—the particular family we're born into, the number of children in it, the quality of our health, and so on. Others—those that are related to biology and society, and the way they have come together in modern times—are shared.

The long dependency of the human infant is a biological fact. The family, and the way it is organized to meet those dependent needs, is a social one. The biological fact of our infantile dependency and the social arrangements designed to care for us through that period are part of our shared estate. The particular experiences that are unique either to our person or to the class, sex, race, or ethnic group into which we are born and will grow give a particular cast to that common background. All are important in our development; all profoundly influence our desires as well as our choices in the years ahead.

But it's our common heritage—biological and social— that summons our attention here. For it leaves us with a shared legacy that must be understood if we are to come to know ourselves and our relationships in ways that will enable us to live together more easily.

About the biological we can do nothing, although how to interpret it and its effects on both infant and mother is still a matter of some debate. Some people argue that the hormonal secretions that attend the birth process are nature's way of creating a bond between mother and child—a bond that ensures the mother's attention, therefore makes the child's survival possible. Others insist that the maternal bonding of which we hear so much these days is itself a social product that has little to do with biological necessity.

It's reassuring to think there's a biological imperative in the mother-infant bond. It makes sense of our social arrangements; it assuages our fears of isolation and loneliness to believe that a powerful bond of nature attaches us to another. But there's nothing in nature, either now or in times past, that requires the kind of emotional attachment that's implied when we speak of this bonding. In fact, historians of the family have presented persuasive evidence to show that the emotional bond between mother and child so familiar to us today was largely nonexistent in earlier historical moments. Edward Shorter, for example, described the common practice among upper-class families in eighteenth-century France of sending their newborn infants away to board with a wet nurse for the first years of life.* And examining parent-child relations in England from the sixteenth through the eighteenth centuries, Lawrence Stone concluded that mothers were "often almost as remote and detached from their infant children as fathers."†

Assuredly, only a woman has the biological capacity to conceive, carry, and birth a child. And once, in another age,

The Making of the Modern Family (New York: Basic Books, 1975).
†*The Family, Sex and Marriage in England 1500–1800* (New York: Harper & Row, 1977), p. 114.

the life of a newborn depended on a woman—although not always a mother, by any means—for food. That, of course, is no longer the case. Today, once we get beyond conception and birth, *mothering* and *fathering*—and all that those words mean to us in terms of the expectations they call up and the imagery they carry—are strictly social constructions, roles we assume because they have been mandated by a set of social conventions so long established and well entrenched that they have come to seem natural to most of us.

Mothering is an all-embracing word. To be mothered is to be nurtured in the most elemental sense—to be cared for in all the ways we might wish or need, from the physical to the psychological. But what does *fathering* mean? It's a much more segmented role, isn't it? It's hard even to think about what it means to be fathered. Words like authority come to mind and, of course, work and the financial support it implies. But there's no larger vision that immediately springs to thought, no yearnings that are stirred by the idea of being fathered as they are by thoughts by being mothered.

There's little doubt that the structure of roles and relationships on which these differences rest defines who we are, how we relate to each other, even how we experience life itself in pervasive and powerful ways. Yet it's difficult to see how these roles could be fixed in nature. Does it make sense that something in nature dictates who supports the family outside the home, who inside; who's smart about money, who about cooking; who can repair a car, who can wash a floor? Even who can nurture a child—who can feed it, clothe it, love it, keep it warm and dry, safe from harm; in essence, who can be the survival figure of that long dependency of the human infant—has nothing to do with biology any longer.

Still, it *is* a fact that a woman, even if not the mother, is almost always the primary caregiver of infancy. *And no fact of our early life has greater consequences for how girls and boys develop into women and men, therefore for how we relate to each other in our adult years.* For, when that social fact is combined with the biological reality of our infantile dependency, the stage is set for developmental consequences of which we have only recently become aware—consequences that are intimately related to the difficulties we encounter in our love relationships and in our marriages.

It isn't that other events and later years are irrelevant or unimportant. Certainly much happens to all of us in the ensuing years that's influential and formative. Without doubt the social and cultural changes of recent years have affected how we view ourselves and each other, how we live together. Yet our years of trying to change ourselves and our relationships have yielded only limited results because we have not yet fully understood that many of the qualities we would change are rooted in our internal world as well as the external one—that we must look to the years from birth to five and to the very structure of parenting itself for their formation. What happens after that can ameliorate the conflicts those differences create between us or it can make them worse. But, since these are the years in which, as we shall see, crucial elements of male and female personality develop, later events cannot take the conflicts away entirely. For all subsequent learning—important though it may be to our development—is layered over those earliest experiences in which a woman is the most important figure in our lives.

If we want to know what contributes to the unique personality traits a person displays, it's to the particular events of life that we would look. "What place did he hold in the family constellation?" we would ask. "What kind of relationships existed between the parents? Between parents and child? What did it mean to be the oldest child in the family? The one in the middle? What was the child's experience when he had to have surgery at eight? When he was caught masturbating at twelve? How did he experience the family's poverty? Their wealth? What was the effect of a divorce? Of a death in the family?" And so on. But, when we want to understand something about men and women at the more general level, something that will teach us why women so uniformly behave one way about certain things, men another, then it's to their shared experience that we look—to their culture, to their biology, to the social institutions within which they live, grow, and work, and to the fact that it is women who mother.

The cultural sources of masculine and feminine personality have been given wide attention in recent years. It's time now to complete the picture—to come to grips with the ways in which one of the most taken for granted parts of our lives, the fact that women mother, is responsible for the creation of the distinct and different personality structures in women and men. Only then can we understand fully how ideology and culture exert such effective control over our lives, why even our best efforts at personal change are met with such difficulty.

To understand how and why it works that way, we must take a short journey into psychological theory. It isn't an easy one—partly because the road is paved with psychological concepts whose meaning is not always patently clear or immediately apparent. But they're essential if we're to go beyond what we already know about the differences between women and men and into a realm of understanding we have not reached before.

The journey starts with Freud. Whatever one may think of psychoanalytic theory, with its development Freud gave us the first clear expression of the fact that adult personality rests on early childhood experience. We may quarrel about some or all of the elements of the theory today, but hardly a murmur is heard to contest the underlying premise on which it is based: We must look to childhood if we are to understand certain central elements of adulthood.

As critics and followers developed and expanded the

original Freudian theory, new understandings emerged about the psychology of infancy. First Melanie Klein, later the theorists of what has come to be known as the British object relations school showed quite convincingly that crucial experiences in the development of a child come much earlier and from a different source than Freud had articulated.* Instead of satisfactory development resting on the successful resolution of the oedipal conflict, as early psychoanalytic theory held, these later theorists came to understand the importance of the pre-oedipal period—the years between birth and five—in the developmental scheme. And, instead of a bundle of instincts and impulses which had to be tamed by parents as the agents of society, they came to see the inner life of a small child as a world made up of what they called "objects." It's an ugly word to use when referring to people and relationships. But they chose it in an attempt

*Melanie Klein, *Contributions to Psycho-analysis,* 1921–1945 (London: Hogarth Press, 1948) and *The Psycho-analysis of Children* (London: Hogarth Press, 1959). While retaining Freud's insistence on instinct as the central determinant of human personality, Klein also developed the basis for what later came to be known as object relations theory. Those who followed in the path she laid out rejected both the instinctual determinism of the earliest psychoanalytic theorists and the cultural determinism of such neo-Freudians as Erich Fromm, Karen Horney, and Clara Thompson. In doing so, they found their way to a dynamic intrapsychic theory of human personality that also takes account of the ways in which culture is incorporated as a crucial part of human development. Object relations theory allows us to understand the interplay between the individual and the society through the medium of the internalization of the external object world and the consequent development of the inner object world. Some major figures in these theoretical developments are Michael Balint, ed., *Primary Love and Psycho-Analytic Technique* (New York: Liveright Publishing, 1965); W. R. D. Fairbairn *An Object-Relations Theory of the Personality* (New York: Basic Books, 1952); Margaret S. Mahler, Fred Pine, and Anni Bergman, *The Psychological Birth of the Human Infant* (New York: Basic Books, 1975); Margaret S. Mahler, *Separation-Individuation* (New York: Jason Aronson, 1979); D. W. Winnicott, *The Family and Individual Development* (New York: Basic Books, 1965) and *The Maturational Processes and the Facilitating Environment* (New York: International Universities Press, 1965).

to make clear that each of these "objects" is not, in fact, a person or even a thing, but an internal *representation* of it as filtered through the child's unique inner experience and consciousness. In ordinary language, then, such "objects" are essentially the mental images we carry inside us—internalizations of people and things that we come to know and identify with.

But what does it mean to internalize something? How can we even know that internalization exists? Can we see it, feel it? The answer is yes. But the experience of it requires us to take a step inside ourselves—to move from the objects of the external world to their representations in our internal one.

At the simplest level, for example, if I say the word "chair," what happens? Immediately we form a mental image of a chair. The *kind* of chair we each see may be different, but the *idea* of "chair" brings to mind the imagery of something to sit on. That's internalization—the mental representation of "chair" we carry inside us.

When we move from things to people, it gets somewhat more complicated because, with a person, there's a relationship involved—a continuing and dynamic interaction in which things both change and remain the same. Consequently, both conscious and unconscious processes are more at issue, and the *meanings* we give to our internal images are at least as important as whatever the external reality might be.

When I say the word "mother," therefore, it calls up a complex response. We may think first of a woman because that's how we have internalized the *idea* of mother, that's how the idea has become symbolized inside us. But there's also a real person who has been mother to each of us. Therefore, we carry inside a representation of her as well—a representation, it must be emphasized, that's not necessarily an accurate rendering of the real person but one we have invested with motives and meanings that may have little to do with reality.

The baby who cries in terror when mother leaves, for example, does so because she or he doesn't yet have the internal development to believe in the existence of what's not immediately present. Therefore, every departure feels like an abandonment—an abandonment that, for a small child, is also a threat to life itself. Mother, of course, returns; for her that was never in doubt. But until the child develops the capacity to carry mother's image inside, there's no certainty for him or her. With that development, separation becomes tolerable. But the fears generated in those early months of life—the sense of mother as powerful, as arbitrary, as wholly in control—do not go away completely. A constant and loving mother may reassure the child and palliate the fears, but the *experience* of the child in those terror-stricken moments leaves its residue in the internalized image of mother.

It's a complicated image, however—formed differently at different stages of development. But each successive formation doesn't obliterate the last one; rather, each is layered over the one before it, the earliest ones living at deeper levels of the unconscious than the later ones. So the mother we experienced in infancy is there beneath the mother of later childhood who lies beneath the one we internalized in adolescence—each of them filtered through the experiences of the developing child in a continuing and complex interaction between the child, the mother, and the needs of both as they were expressed at different developmental points.

This is how it happens that we can catch a glimpse of the real mother at some unexpected moment and find ourselves thinking in surprise, "Why, I never realized she's so small." The experience of her as large and powerful is the internalization of the child; the realization of her actual size comes from the adult who is brought up short by the contradiction between the reality and the unconscious imagery that's thrust into consciousness in an unexpected moment.

This, also, is why, when we think or talk about our own mother, we often surprise ourselves by the contradictory things we say and feel. At one time, she may have been experienced as an all-nurturing mother; at another, as an angry withholding one. We have, therefore, internalized both images and, depending on the circumstances in our adult life, will sometimes experience one as the reality, sometimes the other. But it's the internalized mother of our infancy that will concern us throughout the pages of this book—the image of the one who dominated the years of our childhood from our first days on earth, the years when we were beginning to know and experience the world, to internalize it, if you will.

And how does all this help us to understand our troubled relations with each other? How does it explain the fact that we so often feel like strangers even while living together in close and intimate relationships?

It took the work of Nancy Chodorow, a sociologist, and Dorothy Dinnerstein, a psychologist, to give us the clues.* Standing squarely on the shoulders of the traditions I have sketched so briefly here, and buttressed by the ferment of modern feminist thinking, these writers began to wonder about these "objects" we internalize in infancy, about these

---

*Nancy Chodorow, *The Reproduction of Mothering: Psychoanalysis and the Sociology of Gender* (Berkeley: University of California Press, 1978); Dorothy Dinnerstein, *The Mermaid and the Minotaur: Sexual Arrangements and Human Malaise* (New York: Harper & Row, 1976). My intellectual debt to Nancy Chodorow is especially large. For it was her work, read years before it was published, that opened up for me a new way of seeing the issues that underlie the troubled relations between the sexes. Her concern was to explain how mothering is reproduced in girls; mine has been to show how the differences in male and female personality structure affect crucial parts of the lives of both men and women. But the vision that brought this work to life was born when I first read Chodorow almost ten years ago.

mental representations that become a part of our internal psychic life. And they dared to ask questions never before seriously addressed, the crucial one being: What is the effect on human development of the fact that only women mother? Until they questioned the unquestionable, psychological theory had taken for granted that mother was, and ought to be, the primary parent—that it was the natural destiny of a woman and, if not the only, surely the best road to well-being for a child.

Only recently, then, has the scientific mind been opened to questioning what generally has been believed to be given in nature: the fact that women mother. Even Margaret Mahler's pioneering research deals only with the ways in which maternal care and infant development are related at different stages of the child's growth, never questioning whether the fact that mother is the primary caretaker is itself of crucial developmental significance.* Once that question was asked, however, a whole new range of possibilities was opened before us, and the importance of this fact in accounting for the differences in male and female personality stood revealed.

What follows, then, is a distillation of key aspects of object relations theory as modified by both Chodorow and Dinnerstein, and my own elaboration of that theory which explains not just how the differences between us arise but how they affect our ways of being together in adulthood—especially around such central issues of living and loving as intimacy, sexuality, dependency, work, and parenting.

To understand how it all happens, we go back to infancy. There we see that, from the beginning, life is a process of forming attachments, internalizing representations from the external world, and making identifications with significant people from that world. Since it is mother who is the

*Mahler, Pine, and Bergman, *op. cit.* and Mahler, *op. cit.*

primary caregiver—who feeds us, shelters us, comforts us, holds us in her arms to allay our fears—it is she with whom we make our first attachment, she with whom we form a symbiotic bond within which we do not yet know self from other. For each of us, then, whether a girl or a boy, it is a woman who is in this primary position in our inner life—a woman who is the object of our most profound attachment, a woman who becomes our first loved other.

As the first weeks and months of life pass, this infantile attachment becomes less global, more differentiated. This is the time when we see in the child the first glimmering of the ability to distinguish self from other—and with it, the earliest development of the capacity for identification, for the internalization of another into our inner psychic life.

Identification, in this case, is simply another step in the process of internalization—an extension of it, we might say. In the infant, it signals the beginning of a separate sense of self while, at the same time, forging a new kind of link with mother. It's the first inchoate ability to identify with another as one *like* self. And because a woman has been the primary person in the life of the child until this time, it is with her that this first identification is made. Hers is the imagery that is internalized—the representation that lives inside the small child, the one that the nascent self is measured against.

What this says, then, is that, whether in a girl or a boy, the earliest, most primitive experiences of both attachment and identification are with a woman. We see it in boys of three or four, for example, who say, "When I grow up I'm going to have a baby." Mother intervenes hastily. "No," she'll say, "only girls can have babies." And the small boy bursts into tears of rage and disappointment—feelings born of his inability to understand why, since he has internalized an identification with mother, he can't do what she has done.

Infancy passes; the child leaves the mother's arms,

crawls to the floor, eventually stands straight and walks away. The period of separation and individuation, until now just budding, comes into flower. This is the time when "I" and "you" become more clearly distinguishable to the child, when self and other take on a compelling reality. Thus, it's also the period when the issues of separation and unity come clamorously to the fore—when the child lives in ambivalent oscillation between the desire first for one, then for the other.

It's at once an exciting time for a child and a frightening one, both to be seen quite clearly in any toddler—the triumph as the little one runs off followed by the sudden anxious return. The scene is a familiar one. A small child at play abruptly leaves the toy that a moment earlier had held such fascination, rushes back to mother, climbs onto her lap, holds her tightly, almost urgently. Mother prepares to comfort the little one for a while, only to find herself just as suddenly holding a small mass of wriggling humanity struggling to get away. Reassured of her presence, the child can return to play.

Separation and unity—these are the themes that dominate this period of life. For the child who has had what British psychoanalyst D. W. Winnicott calls "good enough" mothering, the fear that separation means abandonment, the anxiety that outside her presence mother and/or self may cease to exist, will be less acute; for the less fortunate one, more so.

But there is no perfect parenting, no possibility of meeting and assuaging every anxiety a small child experiences. It's simply not in the nature of life, may not even be desirable. Indeed, the parent who seeks to shield a child from the anguish of separation does him or her as much harm as the parent who thrusts the child into separating prematurely. Such misguided attempts at protection may offer some momentary comfort, but they also deprive the child of the joy to be experienced in the developing independence, of the sense of safety that comes with knowing a self exists and can be relied on, of the pleasure of becoming acquainted with that emerging self.

Separation and unity—the excitement and fear, the triumph and anxiety they generate—will remain continuing themes in adult life. How these needs were dealt with when we were small children makes a difference, of course. Depending on our past, they may be more or less powerful, more or less determinate of the kinds of relationships we have with others in our present. But the most we can expect is that they will be less rather than more. And long after the conflict between our need for separation and our desire for unity has left center stage, these issues will live inside us to influence the next act.

Thus, in adulthood, when we find ourselves in an intimate relationship, we each experience again, even if only in highly attenuated form, those early struggles around separation and unity—the conflict between wanting to be one with another and the desire for an independent, autonomous self. For each woman and man who comes into a marriage stirs the yearnings from an unremembered but still powerfully felt past; each brings with her or him two people—the adult who says, "I do," and the child within who once knew both the agony and the ecstasy of a symbiotic union. Ecstasy, because in the mother's arms the infant could experience the bliss of unity and the security that accompanies it. Agony, because from birth onward life seems a series of separations —each one an insistent reminder of those past and those yet to come, each one experienced as a threat to survival itself.

Of course, as adults we know there's no return to the old symbiotic union; of course, survival is no longer at stake in separation. But the child within feels as if this were still the reality. And the adult responds to the archaic memory of those early feelings even though they're very far from consciousness. Thus, we don't usually know what buffets us about—what makes us eager to plunge into a relationship one moment and frightens us into anxious withdrawal the next. We know only that we long for closeness and connection with another, and that we feel unaccountably uncomfortable when we get it—that, without warning, we begin to feel anxious in some ill-defined and indefinable way. A thirty-nine-year-old man I spoke with gave voice to just such feelings.

> Judy and I are close in a way that I'm not close with anyone else. She even knows what I'm thinking a lot of the time. But that's not all a piece of cake. I mean, sometimes I like it that she knows me so well; it's soothing and feels safe. But then there's times when, all of a sudden, I feel like: Christ, I need to get away from her before she eats me up or something. I know it sounds crazy, but it's what it feels like. I don't know why, but when I'm feeling like that, I actually feel like a scared kid. But what am I scared of? Damned if I know!

It is, indeed, hard to know. For it's not the man but the child that still lives inside him who responds this way. It's the child who was mothered by a woman who is now soothed by the belief that, with this woman, too, he's wholly known, completely loved. And the same child who had to separate from mother now withdraws in fear—not just from his wife's expectation of connection but from the seemingly inexhaustible well of his own dependent wishes and needs that this new relationship threatens to reawaken.

The process by which a child separates is a complicated one, including within it several major developmental tasks. Paramount among them is the need to develop an independent, coherent, and continuing sense of self—a self that's unique and separate from any other, one we can recognize as our own, one that can function effectively in the world to get some primary needs met, one that knows an "I" exists irrespective of what happens in a relationship, whether with the mother of infancy or the lover of adult life. This psychological self is the internal analog of our physical self—not visible in the same way, but equally important to our sense of who and what we are.

In this process, two things are central: the crystallization of a gender identity and the maintenance of what psychologists call "ego boundaries"—those personal psychological boundaries of the self that serve to set us off from the rest of the world. This, in large part, is what a child's separation struggle is all about—a struggle that's different for boys and for girls just because it's a woman who has mothered them both.

It's not that the lot of one is easier than the other; growing up is hard for children of either gender. But the problems they encounter with each developmental task are different and, depending upon the issue in process at any given time, are sometimes harder for girls, sometimes for boys. Thus, when the task is to establish the boundaries of self, the identity between mother and daughter make that more complicated for a girl than for a boy. Just because they are the same gender, it's more difficult for a girl to separate, harder for her or her mother to know where one ends and the other begins. On the other hand, when we look at another central issue in this developing selfhood—the establishment of a gender identity, which means the internalization and consolidation of the knowledge that says, "I am a girl"; "I am a boy"—the identity between mother and daughter is a help not a hindrance, while the difference between mother and son makes it a much more difficult and complicated issue for a boy.

It's obvious that the experience of *being* male and *being* female is different. But what has been less clear until now is how the *process* of developing and internalizing a gender identity—so different in girls and in boys because of the structure of parenting—affects the development of ego boundaries and, therefore, determines the shape of feminine and masculine personality in adulthood. *Gender identity* and *ego boundaries*—these are the two elements of self which will be the focus of our attention because these are the two developmental tasks of childhood that are most deeply affected by the fact that women are the primary caregivers of infancy.

Normally the process of gender differentiation starts at birth and continues through the first few years of a child's life. Differences in gender are, of course, biological. But gender *identity* and the *behavior* that flows from it are another matter, as much of the research on the establishment of gender identity shows.* Give a child the wrong gender label for the first years of life and—regardless of what later genital development shows, regardless of serious attempts to correct the error—gender confusion will persist, most likely for life.

When a boy who has been raised by a woman confronts the need to establish his gender identity, it means a profound upheaval in his internal world. Despite the fact that other connections are made during the early months of life—with father, with siblings, with grandparents, even with babysitters—if mother has been the main caregiver, the attachment and the identification with her remain the primary ones. Now, in order to identify with his maleness, he must renounce this connection with the first person outside self to be internalized into his inner psychic world—the one who has been so deeply embedded in his psychic life as to seem a part

*John Money and Anke A. Ehrhardt, *Man and Woman, Boy and Girl* (Baltimore: Johns Hopkins University Press, 1972). Robert J. Stoller, "A Contribution to the Study of Gender Identity," *International Journal of Psycho-Analysis,* Vol. 45 (1964), pp. 220–222; "The Sense of Maleness," *Psychoanalytic Quarterly,* Vol. 34 (1965), pp. 207–218; "The Sense of Femaleness," *Psychoanalytic Quarterly,* Vol. 37 (1968), pp. 42–55; "The Bedrock of Masculinity and Femininity: Bisexuality," *Archives of General Psychiatry,* Vol. 26 (1972), pp. 207–212; "Overview: The Impact of New Advances in Sex Research on Psychoanalytic Theory," *American Journal of Psychiatry,* Vol. 130 (1973), pp. 241–251.

of himself—and seek instead a deeper attachment and identification with father. But this father with whom he is expected to identify has, until this time, been a secondary character in his internal life, often little more than a sometimes
pleasurable, sometimes troublesome shadow on the consciousness of the developing child.*

It's a demanding, complicated, and painful process that
takes its toll on a boy who must grow into a man. Although
they happen at different times in the life of the infant and
are two separate psychological processes, identification and
attachment are so closely linked that the child can't give up
one without an assault on the other. With the repression of
the identification with mother, therefore, the attachment to
her becomes ambivalent. He still needs her, but he can't be
certain anymore that she will be there, that she can be
trusted.

To protect against the pain wrought by this radical shift
in his internal world, he builds a set of defenses that, in
many important ways, will serve him, for good or ill, for the
rest of his life. This is the beginning of the development of
ego boundaries that are fixed and firm—barriers that rigidly
separate self from other, that circumscribe not only his relationships with others but his connection to his inner emotional life as well.

The deprivation he experiences in having to relinquish
this early connection may explain some part of the aggres-

*The question arises: What happens in families where there is no fa-
ther? There will undoubtedly be some differences in individual personali-
ties based on the quality and character of personal experiences, on race,
class, and ethnic background, and the like. But the *process* by which a boy
who has been raised by a woman establishes a gender identity does not
change. Thus, whether a father is actually in the home or not, a boy will
consolidate his gender identity by shifting his primary identification from
a woman to a man. For somewhere inside him there lives an internalized
image of a male—perhaps some other man or men who have touched his
life, perhaps even his idealized representation of the absent father.

siveness that's said to be so natural in men. When directed against women, it can be understood as a response to that early loss, and to the sense of betrayal that went with it. For, as a child, his inner experience is not that he did something but that something was done to him—that this mother who had, until then, been the loved adult on whom he could count, with whom he could identify, abandoned him to the shadowy and alien world of men. How, then, could she—or any woman—ever be wholly trusted again?

Whether true in the literal sense or not is irrelevant; it's the way the experience is internalized and understood by the child that counts. In this sense, the need for such repression engenders feelings of abandonment that are, in themselves, enough to stimulate plenty of rage. But it seems to me that we are witness also to a case of aggression turned outward in an attempt to compensate for the original aggression that was turned inward when, as a small child, he had to sunder his inner life so ruthlessly.

Parenthetically, it's in this developmental sequence that we can make sense of the contempt for women we see so often among men. If we consider the dilemma of the small boy and the internal rupture this separation requires, we can understand that the contempt is born of fear, not arrogance —the fear of a child who finds himself pressed to reject so powerful an inner presence as mother has been in his early life. It's a fear so great that he can live with it only by disempowering her—by convincing himself that she's a weak and puny creature whose lack of maleness must doom her forever to a subordinate and contemptible place in the world.

Difficult though the development of a separate and independent self may be for a boy, there are differences between himself and his mother that help the boundaries to become sharp and clear. He is, after all, anatomically male; she, female. In fact, it seems reasonable to speculate that men's self-conscious concern with their penis as an organ of identity originates in these early years. It makes sense, doesn't it? When, as a small child, the time comes for a boy to separate himself from mother in favor of an identification with a man, what else can he do to give some reality to the task ahead; how else can he make reasonable this demand that feels so *un*reasonable?

For girls, the process of developing an independent sense of self presents a wholly different set of obstacles. It's another of those contradictions that makes this developmental tale so elusive and so provocative. Just as the fact that there are no obvious differences between a girl and her mother makes the process of establishing a gender identity easier for girls than for boys, the problem of separating—of defining and experiencing self as an autonomous, bounded individual—is harder.

In the normal developmental course, the formation of a gender identity in a girl requires no wrenching breaks with the past. She's a girl, mother's a woman; the one, she understands intuitively, leads quite naturally to the other. Since she need not displace the internalized representation of the loved mother, there's no need to build defenses against feeling and attachment, therefore, no need for the kind of rigid boundaries a man develops as a means of protecting and maintaining those defenses. This means that, as a woman, she'll develop ego boundaries that are more permeable than a man's—a fact of paramount importance in the management of both her internal life and her external one.

It is in this part of the developmental scenario that we see the birth of the empathic capacities for which women are so justly known. The context within which separation takes place and identity is forged means that a girl never has to separate herself as completely and irrevocably as a boy must. Her sense of herself, therefore, is never as separate as his; she experiences herself always as more continuous with another; and the maintenance of close personal connections will continue to be one of life's essential themes for her. As a result, she will preserve the capacity, born in the early symbiotic union, for participating in another's inner life, for sensing another's emotional states almost as if they were her own—the capacity that, in an adult, we call empathy.

For the same reasons, a girl develops a more complex internal life than a boy. As she grows toward maturity, she not only retains her identification with mother as a vital part of her inner life, she internalizes father as a loved other as well. This process takes place much later, long after gender identity has been consolidated. But it is, nevertheless, central to an understanding of the differences in the internal life of a woman and a man. For, when a boy internalizes father and banishes mother, he is left with only one significant other who is actively experienced in his inner psychic life, only one with whom he must negotiate. For a girl, there are two. It may not seem like much, but the difference in psychic structure, therefore in personality development, is enormous. For it means that a woman's inner relational negotiations become triangular while a man's remain dyadic.

It should be clear that mother does not disappear entirely from the inner life of a boy. Indeed, it may even look as if all is the same, since in conscious life she remains an important and obvious presence. At the unconscious level, however, the identification is repressed, the internalized image undergoes a radical change, and he begins to build defenses against the needs, wishes, and feelings that are associated with that early relationship. But no matter how high the walls, no matter how tough the defensive structure, the conflict created by the repression continues to make itself felt. We see its expression, for example, in the resentment that adult men often feel at the birth of their first child.

It's not that such men don't want the child, not that there's no satisfaction in fatherhood for them, not that they don't take some real pleasure in this new addition in the family. But alongside whatever positive feelings they may have lie the others—those feelings that arise unbidden out of that unremembered but painful past, out of the need to repress the first loved other, out of the deep sense of loss such repression begets, and out of the child's anger at a mother who failed to protect him from that hurt.

For some men, the birth of a child activates the fear of being abandoned once again: "It felt like she just left me, she just wasn't there for me." For others, there's the reminder of an older loss: "I didn't know I remembered it until Bobby was born, but it was the same feelings I had when my younger brother came along. It was never the same with my mother after that." Or there's the reawakening of a very old competition, especially if the infant happens to be a boy: "I know it sounds awful, but it's like having a competitor. I have to compete with the baby for her time and attention. And it makes it worse because she's so into the whole damn mothering bit—you know, nursing him and all, she really gets off on it."

We're puzzled by such men, condemn their behavior. We wonder aloud how grown men can be jealous of a helpless child; we give their feelings a pejorative or pathological label. Yet it seems like an outcome we could anticipate, given the developmental tasks that the current arrangements in the family impose on a boy. For the repression of the identification with mother and the consequent damage to the attachment haven't ended the matter for him. Quite the opposite. Repression can drive the banished wishes and needs into his unconscious, but they live there to demand a hearing another day. Thus, the yearning for the repressed part will continue to make itself felt, pushing him to recreate the archaic infantile situation in adulthood in the hope that, this time, the outcome will be a different one. This means that he'll probably spend the rest of his life trying to re-establish that first exclusive relationship with another while also struggling with his ambivalence about the attachment— swinging between his wariness of emotional connection and his wish to find again that early ecstatic experience with a woman.

When he marries, he takes comfort in having found again the union with a woman he had to renounce so long ago. When the first child arrives, however, all he has longed for and finally acquired is threatened once more—the exclusive relationship lost, the dream disrupted. So he retreats— angry at his wife, demanding, competitive, jealous of his own child, while also ashamed of these feelings inside him that he doesn't understand, certainly doesn't welcome. Recalling just such an unhappy set of circumstances, a thirty-year-old father said:

> I had been lonely for a long time—a long time. Then when Ellen and I got married, it changed. I finally had someone in my life who was really there for me. I was a little intimidated about the idea of marriage before we did it—you know, I was worried about my independence and things like that. But, once we decided, I can't explain what happened to me; it was like coming home again.
>
> Those first two years were almost perfect. Even her pregnancy was great. But when the kid was born everything changed; it sort of all fell apart. It seemed like she was busy with him all the time. And I felt like I didn't count anymore. It was like the bottom fell out of everything, and I got resentful of Danny, then I felt terrible. What kind of father am I to feel angry at a little kid like that? But I couldn't help how I felt. I hated it; I hated the whole damned thing, but I couldn't help it. It was too late. He was here and it felt like things would never be the same again for me and Ellen. There'd never be just the two of us again.

"It was like coming home again," he says. And as in that other life, that other home, an exclusive relationship with a woman is gone—the pain of that old loss making even more intensely poignant the experience of this new one.

For his wife, his response is a troubling one. "How can he feel this way about his own child?" she keeps asking herself. She knows the intensity of her feelings for this baby and wonders, "How can it be so different for him than for me?" She may try to comfort him, to offer some reassurance, but she's angry also—not because she's unfeeling, uncaring, or somehow so immersed in the infant that her husband has ceased to matter, but because she simply cannot understand.

Even when they try to speak to each other about their differences, they can't really "hear." Partly that's because there's a certain reality to a man's perception that's difficult for his wife to grasp. Mothering makes claims upon a woman in a way that fathering, in its traditional form, does not. For the young father, therefore, there *is* a loss—the loss of his wife's exclusive attention, of some of the time they spent together; the loss also of some of the intensity in their relationship as she devotes herself to the care of the new infant.

The new mother, too, may feel some diminution in the intensity of her relationship with her husband, may regret the lessening of the time that's available to spend with him. But offsetting whatever difficulties such changes may present is her deep involvement and connection with the infant, her excitement in their developing relationship—a relationship from which fathers so often are excluded. Partly that's because the traditional role divisions in the family make a father a nonessential parent at this stage of a child's life; and partly it's because men themselves often have difficulty in relating to the helplessness of an infant.

And there's something else as well. For a woman has difficulty understanding her husband's possessiveness and need for exclusivity precisely because of the triangular configuration of her inmost psychic life. It's here that we can see the source of a woman's relative ease with both new baby and husband. This is the internal constellation that equips women for the kind of complex negotiation of relationships

in the external world for which they are known. We see it all
the time: women whose exquisitely tuned ability to find their
way around the world of human relationships enables them
to navigate the emotional demands of a variety of relationships with considerably more comfort and ease than is possible for men. Thus, they become the emotional managers in
the family—interpreting fathers and children to each other,
siblings to one another, keeping extended family relationships in good order, maintaining the family friendships as
well as their own.

For a woman, then, the sameness with mother, and the
continuity of identification it permits, enables the development of these capacities. For a man, difference and discon-
tinuity dominate the early developmental period and,
therefore, disable the growth of these same qualities. It's
true that many men consider themselves too busy or too important to attend to such mundane matters. But alongside
that truth lies another one that has been less apparent to
most of us. For, in reality, most men are not very good at
interpersonal negotiations that are laden with emotional
content because their inner relational life was left relatively impoverished by the need to repress their early primary identification with mother. Therefore, they turn their
attention to those matters they can do well—managing
those aspects of life such as work and finances that seem to
be more subject to rational control—and call those important to cover their incapacity in those things their wives do
so well. But it isn't, as lore would have it, that women are
"doing what comes naturally." Rather, their acuity in these
matters is a product of the process I've been talking about,
which itself is the result of the fact that it's only women
who mother.

These are the parameters within which we struggle to
relate to each other. For women, the issue of maintaining
separation dominates; for men, it's sustaining unity that's so

difficult—problems that make themselves felt around every important issue in a marriage, from the conflicts we experience around intimacy and dependency to the way we parent our children.

(4)

The Approach-Avoidance Dance
Men, Women, and Intimacy

*For one human being to love another, that is
perhaps the most difficult of all our tasks, the
ultimate, the last test and proof, the work for
which all other work is but preparation.*

RAINER MARIA RILKE

INTIMACY. WE HUNGER FOR IT, but we also fear it. We come
close to a loved one, then we back off. A teacher I had once
described this as the "go away a little closer" message. I call
it the approach-avoidance dance.

The conventional wisdom says that women want intimacy, men resist it. And I have plenty of material that would
seem to support that view. Whether in my research interviews, in my clinical hours, or in the ordinary course of my
life, I hear the same story told repeatedly. "He doesn't talk to
me," says a woman. "I don't know what she wants me to talk
about," says a man. "I want to know what he's feeling," she
tells me. "I'm not feeling anything," he insists. "Who can feel
nothing?" she cries. "I can," he shouts. As the heat rises, so
does the wall between them. Defensive and angry, they retreat—stalemated by their inability to understand each
other.

Women complain to each other all the time about not
being able to talk to their men about the things that matter
most to them—about what they themselves are thinking and
feeling, about what goes on in the hearts and minds of the
men they're relating to. And men, less able to expose them-

selves and their conflicts—those within themselves or those with the women in their lives—either turn silent or take cover by holding women up to derision. It's one of the norms of male camaraderie to poke fun at women, to complain laughingly about the mystery of their minds, wonderingly about their ways. Even Freud did it when, in exasperation, he asked mockingly, "What do women want? Dear God, what do they want?"

But it's not a joke—not for the women, not for the men who like to pretend it is.

> The whole goddamn business of what you're calling intimacy bugs the hell out of me. I never know what you women mean when you talk about it. Karen complains that I don't talk to her, but it's not talk she wants, it's some other damn thing, only I don't know what the hell it is. Feelings, she keeps asking for. So what am I supposed to do if I don't have any to give her or to talk about just because she decides it's time to talk about feelings? Tell me, will you; maybe we can get some peace around here.

The expression of such conflicts would seem to validate the common understandings that suggest that women want and need intimacy more than men do—that the issue belongs to women alone; that, if left to themselves, men would not suffer it. But things are not always what they seem. And I wonder: "If men would renounce intimacy, what is their stake in relationships with women?"

Some would say that men need women to tend to their daily needs—to prepare their meals, clean their houses, wash their clothes, rear their children—so that they can be free to attend to life's larger problems. And, given the traditional structure of roles in the family, it has certainly worked that way most of the time. But, if that were all men seek, why is it that, even when they're not relating to women, so much of their lives is spent in search of a relationship with another, so much agony experienced when it's not available?

These are difficult issues to talk about—even to think about—because the subject of intimacy isn't just complicated, it's slippery as well. Ask yourself: What is intimacy? What words come to mind, what thoughts?

It's an idea that excites our imagination, a word that seems larger than life to most of us. It lures us, beckoning us with a power we're unable to resist. And, just because it's so seductive, it frightens us as well—seeming sometimes to be some mysterious force from outside ourselves that, if we let it, could sweep us away.

But what is it we fear?

Asked what intimacy is, most of us—men and women—struggle to say something sensible, something that we can connect with the real experience of our lives. "Intimacy is knowing there's someone who cares about the children as much as you do." "Intimacy is a history of shared experience." "It's sitting there having a cup of coffee together and watching the eleven-o'clock news." "It's knowing you care about the same things." "It's knowing she'll always understand." "It's him sitting in the hospital for hours at a time when I was sick." "It's knowing he cares when I'm hurting." "It's standing by me when I was out of work." "It's seeing each other at our worst." "It's sitting across the breakfast table." "It's talking when you're in the bathroom." "It's knowing we'll begin and end each day together."

These seem the obvious things—the things we expect when we commit our lives to one another in a marriage, when we decide to have children together. And they're not to be dismissed as inconsequential. They make up the daily experience of our lives together, setting the tone for a relationship in important and powerful ways. It's sharing such commonplace, everyday events that determines the temper and the texture of life, that keeps us living together even when other aspects of the relationship seem less than perfect. Knowing someone is there, is constant, and can be counted on in just the ways these thoughts express provides the background of emotional security and stability we look for when we enter a marriage. Certainly a marriage and the people in it will be tested and judged quite differently in an unusual situation or in a crisis. But how often does life present us with circumstances and events that are so out of the range of ordinary experience?

These ways in which a relationship feels intimate on a daily basis are only one part of what we mean by intimacy, however—the part that's most obvious, the part that doesn't awaken our fears. At a lecture where I spoke of these issues recently, one man commented also, "Intimacy is putting aside the masks we wear in the rest of our lives." A murmur of assent ran through the audience of a hundred or so. Intuitively we say "yes." Yet this is the very issue that also complicates our intimate relationships.

On the one hand, it's reassuring to be able to put away the public persona—to believe we can be loved for who we *really* are, that we can show our shadow side without fear, that our vulnerabilities will not be counted against us. "The most important thing is to feel I'm accepted just the way I am," people will say.

But there's another side. For, when we show ourselves thus without the masks, we also become anxious and fearful. "Is it possible that someone could love the *real* me?" we're likely to ask. Not the most promising question for the further development of intimacy, since it suggests that, whatever else another might do or feel, it's we who have trouble loving ourselves. Unfortunately, such misgivings are not usually experienced consciously. We're aware only that our discomfort has risen, that we feel a need to get away. For the person who has seen the "real me" is also the one who reflects back to us an image that's usually not wholly to our liking. We get angry at that, first at ourselves for not living up to our own expectations, then at the other, who becomes for us the mirror of our self-doubts—a displacement of hostility that serves intimacy poorly.

There's yet another level—one that's further below the surface of consciousness, therefore, one that's much more difficult for us to grasp, let alone to talk about. I'm referring to the differences in the ways in which women and men deal with their inner emotional lives—differences that create barriers between us that can be high indeed. It's here that we see how those early childhood experiences of separation and individuation—the psychological tasks that were required of us in order to separate from mother, to distinguish ourselves as autonomous persons, to internalize a firm sense of gender identity—take their toll on our intimate relationships.

Stop a woman in mid-sentence with the question, "What are you feeling right now?" and you might have to wait a bit while she reruns the mental tape to capture the moment just passed. But, more than likely, she'll be able to do it successfully. More than likely, she'll think for a while and come up with an answer.

The same is not true of a man. For him, a similar question usually will bring a sense of wonderment that one would even ask it, followed quickly by an uncomprehending and puzzled response. "What do you mean?" he'll ask. "I was just talking," he'll say.

I've seen it most clearly in the clinical setting where the task is to get to the feeling level—or, as one of my male patients said when he came into therapy, to "hook up the head and the gut." Repeatedly when therapy begins, I find myself having to teach a man how to monitor his internal states—how to attend to his thoughts and feelings, how to bring them into consciousness. In the early stages of our work, it's a common experience to say to a man, "How does that feel?", and to see a blank look come over his face. Over and over, I find myself listening as a man speaks with calm reason about a situation which I know must be fraught with pain. "How do you feel about that?" I'll ask. "I've just been telling you," he's likely to reply. "No," I'll say, "you've told me what happened, not how you *feel* about it." Frustrated, he might well respond, "You sound just like my wife."

It would be easy to write off such dialogues as the problems of men in therapy, of those who happen to be having some particular emotional difficulties. But it's not so, as any woman who has lived with a man will attest. Time and again women complain: "I can't get him to verbalize his feelings." "He talks, but it's always intellectualizing." "He's so closed off from what he's feeling, I don't know how he lives that way." "If there's one thing that will eventually ruin this marriage, it's the fact that he can't talk about what's going on inside him." "I have to work like hell to get anything out of him that resembles a feeling that's something besides anger. That I get plenty of—me and the kids, we all get his anger. Anything else is damn hard to come by with him." One woman talked eloquently about her husband's anguish over his inability to get problems in his work life resolved. When I asked how she knew about his pain, she answered:

> I pull for it, I pull hard, and sometimes I can get something from him. But it'll be late at night in the dark—you know, when we're in bed and I can't look at him while he's talking and he doesn't have to look at me. Otherwise, he's just defensive and puts on what I call his bear act, where he makes his warning, go-away faces, and he can't be reached or penetrated at all.

To a woman, the world men live in seems a lonely one —a world in which their fears of exposing their sadness and pain, their anxiety about allowing their vulnerability to show, even to a woman they love, is so deeply rooted inside them that, most often, they can only allow it to happen "late at night in the dark."

Yet, if we listen to what men say, we will hear their insistence that they *do* speak of what's inside them, *do* share their thoughts and feelings with the women they love. "I tell her, but she's never satisfied," they complain. "No matter how much I say, it's never enough," they grumble.

From both sides, the complaints have merit. The problem lies not in what men don't say, however, but in what's not there—in what, quite simply, happens so far out of consciousness that it's not within their reach. For men have integrated all too well the lessons of their childhood—the experiences that taught them to repress and deny their inner thoughts, wishes, needs, and fears; indeed, not even to notice them. It's real, therefore, that the kind of inner thoughts and feelings that are readily accessible to a woman generally are unavailable to a man. When he says, "I don't know what I'm feeling," he isn't necessarily being intransigent and withholding. More than likely, he speaks the truth.

Partly that's a result of the ways in which boys are trained to camouflage their feelings under cover of an exterior of calm, strength, and rationality. Fears are not manly. Fantasies are not rational. Emotions, above all, are not for the strong, the sane, the adult. Women suffer them, not men —women, who are more like children with what seems like their never-ending preoccupation with their emotional life. But the training takes so well because of their early childhood experience when, as very young boys, they had to shift their identification from mother to father and sever themselves from their earliest emotional connection. Put the two together and it does seem like suffering to men to have to experience that emotional side of themselves, to have to give it voice.

This is the single most dispiriting dilemma of relations between women and men. He complains, "She's so emotional, there's no point in talking to her." She protests, "It's him you can't talk to, he's always so darned rational." He says, "Even when I tell her nothing's the matter, she won't quit." She says, "How can I believe him when I can see with my own eyes that something's wrong?" He says, "Okay, so something's wrong! What good will it do to tell her?" She cries, "What are we married for? What do you need me for, just to wash your socks?"

These differences in the psychology of women and men are born of a complex interaction between society and the individual. At the broadest social level is the rending of thought and feeling that is such a fundamental part of Western thought. Thought, defined as the ultimate good, has been assigned to men; feeling, considered at best a problem, has fallen to women.

So firmly fixed have these ideas been that, until recently, few thought to question them. For they were built into the structure of psychological thought as if they spoke to an eternal, natural, and scientific truth. Thus, even such a great and innovative thinker as Carl Jung wrote, "The woman is increasingly aware that love alone can give her her full stature, just as the man begins to discern that spirit alone can endow his life with its highest meaning. Fundamentally, therefore, both seek a psychic relation one to the other, because love needs the spirit, and the spirit love, for their fulfillment."*

For a woman, "love"; for a man, "spirit"—each expected to complete the other by bringing to the relationship the missing half. In German, the word that is translated here as spirit is *Geist.* But *The New Cassell's German Dictionary* shows that another primary meaning of *Geist* is "mind, intellect, intelligence, wit, imagination, sense of reason." And, given the context of these words, it seems reasonable that *Geist* for Jung referred to a man's highest essence—his

*Carl Gustav Jung, *Contributions to Analytical Psychology* (New York: Harcourt, Brace & Co., 1928), p. 185.

mind. There's no ambiguity about a woman's calling, however. It's love.

Intuitively, women try to heal the split that these definitions of male and female have foisted upon us.

> I can't stand that he's so damned unemotional and expects me to be the same. He lives in his head all the time, and he acts like anything that's emotional isn't worth dealing with.

Cognitively, even women often share the belief that the rational side, which seems to come so naturally to men, is the more mature, the more desirable.

> I know I'm too emotional, and it causes problems between us. He can't stand it when I get emotional like that. It turns him right off.

Her husband agrees that she's "too emotional" and complains:

> Sometimes she's like a child who's out to test her parents. I have to be careful when she's like that not to let her rile me up because otherwise all hell would break loose. You just can't reason with her when she gets like that.

It's the rational-man–hysterical-woman script, played out again and again by two people whose emotional repertoire is so limited that they have few real options. As the interaction between them continues, she reaches for the strongest tools she has, the mode she's most comfortable and familiar with: She becomes progressively more emotional and expressive. He falls back on his best weapons: He becomes more rational, more determinedly reasonable. She cries for him to attend to her feelings, whatever they may be. He tells her coolly, with a kind of clenched-teeth reasonableness, that it's silly for her to feel that way, that she's just being emotional. And of course she is. But that dismissive word "just" is the last straw. She gets so upset that she does, in fact, seem hysterical. He gets so bewildered by the whole interaction that his only recourse is to build the wall of reason even higher. All of which makes things measurably worse for both of them.

> The more I try to be cool and calm her the worse it gets. I swear, I can't figure her out. I'll keep trying to tell her not to get so excited, but there's nothing I can do. Anything I say just makes it worse. So then I try to keep quiet, but . . . wow, the explosion is like crazy, just nuts.

And by then it *is* a wild exchange that any outsider would agree was "just nuts." But it's not just her response that's off, it's his as well—their conflict resting in the fact that we equate the emotional with the nonrational.

This notion, shared by both women and men, is a product of the fact that they were born and reared in this culture. But there's also a difference between them in their capacity to apprehend the *logic* of emotions—a difference born in their early childhood experiences in the family, when boys had to repress so much of their emotional side and girls could permit theirs to flower.

For men, generally the idea of the "logic of emotions" seems a contradiction in terms. For women, it's not. The complexity of their inner life—their relatively easy shifts between the intuitive and the cognitive, the emotional and the rational—provides some internal evidence with which to stand in opposition to the ideology the culture propounds so assiduously. So they both believe and disbelieve it all at once. They believe because it's so difficult to credit their own experience in the face of such a cultural assault. And they disbelieve because it's also so difficult to completely discredit that same experience. Thus, a woman will say:

> When he gets into that oh-so-reasonable place, there are times when I feel like I'm going crazy. Well, I don't know if I'm really nuts, but I'm plenty hysterical. When I can get a hold of myself, I can tell myself it's not me, it's him, that he's

driving me crazy because he refuses to listen to what I'm saying and behaves as if I'm talking in Turkish or something.

All this, however, tells us only about the differences between men and women in how accessible their inner thoughts are to them. There remains the question: When they're available, how willing are they to speak those thoughts to one another?

"The word," wrote Thomas Mann in *The Magic Mountain*, "even the most contradictory word, preserves contact —it is silence which isolates." Words that go right to a woman's heart. For her, intimacy without words is small comfort most of the time. It's not that she needs always to talk, but it's important to her to know what's going on inside him if she's to feel close. And it's equally important for her to believe he cares about what's going on inside her. Thus a vivacious thirty-one-year-old woman, married six years, said:

> It's always the same. I'm the one who tries to get things going. I'm always doing my bla-bla-bla number, you know, keeping things moving and alive around here. But he's the original Mr. Shutmouth most of the time, so I'd just as leave be with a friend and I go call somebody up and talk to her for a while. At least she cares about what I have to say, and she always has something to say back. Then—I swear, I don't know why it bothers him because he wasn't talking to me or noticing me or anything—but anyway, then he gets mad at me, or jealous or something, for talking on the telephone.

That, too, is a familiar tale, the cycle the same in family after family. Women have long conversations on the phone with friends; men are angered by it; women complain uncomprehendingly:

> I can never understand why he gets upset; it's not as if I'm taking anything from him when I get on the phone. Most of the time we haven't said a word to each other in hours.

For a man, it's reassuring just to be in a woman's presence again—to know that, like the mother of infancy, she's there and available when and as she's needed. Then, in that distant past, he didn't need words to feel soothed and comforted; mother's presence was enough. To recreate that experience in adulthood is to heal some of the pain of childhood. Words, therefore, are less important than proximity itself.

Obviously, I don't mean to suggest that men wholly devalue words and their importance to a relationship. But it's equally plain that they will often see difficulties about talking where women will not. For example, some men worry that talking about a problem will escalate it by giving the feelings that underlie it more concrete form. When a woman wants to discuss some issue in their relationship, therefore, her husband may demur out of fear. One thirty-eight-year-old electrician gave voice to those concerns with as clear a statement as I have ever heard:

> She wants to talk about something that worries her—maybe something between us—but it makes me nervous so I don't want to hear about it. As soon as she starts talking about her worries, she exaggerates the problem, and all of a sudden, we've got a big nut on our hands. Who needs it? So lots of times when she starts, I'll back off, figuring her talking is only going to make it worse. [With a crooked smile] But that doesn't work so well either because then she gets mad because I don't want to hear and then *that's* the problem. It's no win!

But this is only a specific example of the more general theme—the fact that connecting words with feeling and emotion is difficult and frightening for most men. It's difficult because the repression came so early in life—at the stage before the linguistic ability to express complex feelings had fully developed—thereby creating an internal split between the two. And it's frightening because the verbal expression of emotion seems to them to threaten to provoke conflict or to expose vulnerability.

Words, therefore, are not at the center of the definition of intimacy for most men; nonverbal activities will do for them at least as well, often better. Thus, the husband who is accused of being "Mr. Shutmouth" complains:

> She objects because I do a lot of reading, and she keeps hassling me that I don't talk to her enough. She tells me all the time we can't be really close if we're not talking to each other. It's hard for me to understand what she means. Doesn't she know that it feels close to me just to be in the same room with her? I tell her, but all I get back is more of her talk. Jesus, I get so tired of hearing words all the time. I don't understand how women can nag a subject to death.

His wife counters:

> Carl's always surprised that my friends and I have so much to talk about. But that's exactly what I would want from him. I'd like him to *want* to talk about all his thoughts and feelings with me. I mean, I'd love to be able to dissect and obsess over all the emotional issues in his life with him like I do with my friends.
>
> He says I need to live every experience at least twice—once in the living and then in talking about it. And I think he's right. [With mounting irritation] But what's wrong with that? Why can't I get him to share the reliving of it, or examination or whatever you want to call it, like I can do with any of my women friends?

On the other side are the men who insist they talk plenty, who say they're quite willing to share their thoughts with the woman they love but that, all too often, she has trouble listening. Thus this complaint from a twenty-nine-year-old salesman in a five-year marriage:

> Our problem is not my talking but getting her to listen, I mean, to pay attention. It's like she drifts off when I'm trying to tell her how I feel about something, then I get mad as hell. First she complains I don't talk, then when I do, she disappears somewhere in her head.

His wife has another story:

> He says he's telling me how he feels, but he doesn't want anything from me—just that I'm expected to be there listening to every word. It's like dealing with my three-year-old. He wants to talk to me, too.

Puzzled, I said, "I'm not sure I understand what you mean. Could you explain it to me?" She sat quietly, thinking for a while, then:

> Well, when Jason—that's my son—comes running to talk to me, he doesn't want anything from me, he just wants me to be there to listen to him. That's what mommies are for. He'll come to cry if he hurts himself or to show me something he's excited about, but it's not what you could call two people communicating with each other. There's this little kid who wants his mommy's attention—you know, to fix the hurt or . . . Oh hell, I don't know what—just to be there, I guess. Well, it's kind of the same thing with Paul. First of all, he's not talking *to* me, he's saying words *at* me. I mean, he doesn't want a *conversation*, he just wants to talk—like a kid who comes running to mom, has his say, and then goes away again without ever paying any attention to the person underneath the mommy. Do you know what I mean?

Her experience at such times is that these are not intimate moments, but covert expressions of his dependency. And it makes her both angry and lonely. It's all right to be "mommy" to the child; from the father she wants something else. Sometimes she tells him:

> I try to tell him that I don't want it to be all on his timetable. When he's ready to say something, we can talk. But why doesn't he care about me and my timetable; why doesn't he ask about how I'm feeling or what I'm thinking? Oh, sure, if I get real mad or hysterical or something, he'll notice. But otherwise . . . you have to hit him over the head. I sometimes feel like I've got two kids, not one. And I tell him, too, but he doesn't really get it. [More gently] I think he tries, but he doesn't get it.

It is, indeed, hard for him to understand the message she keeps trying to convey, hard to know just what she wants and how to give it to her.

> She says lots of times when I want to talk to her that it's the same as Jason wanting her attention. But I don't know what she's talking about, and she's never been able to explain it to me.

What she's asking from him is a sharing of his inner life and thoughts not out of fear, not out of a need to be cared for, but out of the wish to expose that part of himself. But that alone wouldn't satisfy either, because along with his own openness she wants him to *want* hers. She doesn't want to have to ask him to listen to her innermost thoughts, she wants him to *want* to know them. That's one important definition of intimacy among adults—the wish to know another's inner life along with the ability to share one's own.

But we all know couples today who are struggling against such stereotypic ways of being and of living together. Perhaps we ourselves are among them. And sometimes, happily, we win the battle to free ourselves from our past. Then, at some unexpected moment when the guard is relaxed, we find ourselves caught again, as the story of this interaction between husband and wife tells so eloquently.

He's a musician; she manages a gift shop. At thirty-six and thirty-three respectively, they have been married for eight years and are the parents of two children aged four and six. His words come quickly, the tension evident not just in his voice but in the set of his head, in the furrowed brow that fits well with the anxious smile that comes and goes, in the taut way he leans forward in the chair.

> It hasn't been easy to work on this intimacy stuff because it sometimes feels like we're so far apart. But I think we're both getting better at it. I really try to tell her what's going on in my mind more. [Sighing] But it can still be damned hard; even

when I know what I'm thinking, it's hard as hell to say it sometimes. I've tried to tell her that I'm not just being stubborn or hostile; I actually feel scared at times like that.

"What are you scared of?" I asked. He stared out the window for a bit, then, with some agitation, said:

Damned if I know. It's like a kid in a way—scared I'll say or do the wrong thing and wind up in trouble, so better to just hole up and keep quiet.

The wife, a tall, auburn-haired woman, spoke more calmly, weighing her words carefully as if trying to be sure she would portray the issues fairly.

I don't think anything is more difficult for us than this business of trying to be open. [Stops for a moment wanting to clarify her position, then] Look, I want you to understand that I'm not one of these people who thinks openness or honesty in a relationship means spilling your guts or telling your partner every angry thought that comes into your head. There's plenty I don't talk about—like when I wonder do I really love him sometimes, or do I want to be married. Those things don't have to be said; they're damaging. But . . . how can I say it, it's the real stuff that goes on in him I want to know about. I mean, I want him to be able to say something hurts him or scares him, not just to barricade himself off behind the paper or something.

But I've had to learn that I can't have it all my way. I have to let him come to it without my constant pushing all the time. And when it comes to a certain kind of sharing of your innards and examining it, maybe I have to know that I'll never get from him what I get from Sally—she's my closest friend. I also think I've come to understand better now that there are things I get from Stephen that I don't get from anyone else. [Laughing] Who else would put up with my moods and all the crap I put out in this relationship? So now, when I get upset and begin to feel sorry for myself because Sally knows me better than Stephen in some ways, I remind myself pretty quick that he knows me better than she does in other ways, and that maybe he has to put up with the worst part of me.

I guess the important thing we both feel is that we're

growing and changing. [Again, an ironic laugh] It's just not like in the storybooks or the fantasies but, well . . . what is?

The husband:

We keep trying, but I've got to tell you, sometimes nothing works. I don't know what happens, but something gets going in me and there's no stopping it.

"Tell me about that," I prompted, as his hesitation became apparent.

Well, it can go something like this. Molly can come into the room, take one look, and know something's wrong. So she'll ask: "What's the matter?" And then the craziest damn thing happens. Instead of saying, "I'm feeling really terrible, and I need to talk to you," what do I do? I stick my head deeper into the paper I'm reading and grunt something unintelligible. She'll say again, "Hey, what's the matter? Is anything wrong?" I'll just mutter, "Nothing." Then she'll say, "It doesn't sound like nothing; you sound angry at me. Are you?" I'll say, "I'm not angry at you." But the truth is, the vibes say I'm sitting there smoldering. But I don't give an inch. It's like she's going to take something priceless from me, that's how hard I hold on to it. [Hunching his shoulders and leaning still further forward] But I don't even know what the "it" is. I just know it's like when my mother would keep harping on me: "Where you going? What you doing? Who you seeing?" It's really nuts. There's some part of me that doesn't *want* her to leave me alone, like I want her to push me so maybe I won't feel so bad. But when she does I freeze up, like I have to protect myself from her.

It's inevitable, however, that the withdrawal will soon exact its price, that the other side of his ambivalent strivings will emerge. The child within clamors to be attended, to be cared for, to be reassured. He reaches out to his wife, who, by now, has retreated into her own hostile silence because his withdrawal feels so rejecting to her. He responds with disappointment, fear, then anger—each following the other in quick succession.

> When she finally goes away—no, she doesn't just go, I drive her
> away. Anyway, she leaves, and for a minute I feel better—like,
> "Aha, I made her suffer too." But it doesn't last long because
> I begin to feel like a jerk for how I've been acting. And I trash
> myself for feeling bad and for not having the strength to cope
> the way I should. I guess I get a little scared, too, that maybe
> she'll leave permanently. So I make a move. But by then she's
> having none of it.

Eventually husband and wife wind up in a fight. In such
situations, it makes no difference what the adults actually
say to each other as they fight it out, for it's the children who
are playing out an old conflict that has nothing to do with the
substance the grown-ups have given it.

> From there on, it's downhill all the way. She's mad, then I
> have a good reason to be mad instead of whatever the hell I
> was feeling that started the whole mess. And away we go.

It should be understood: Commitment itself is not a problem for a man; he's good at that. He can spend a lifetime
living in the same family, working at the same job—even one
he hates. And he's not without an inner emotional life. But
when a relationship requires the sustained verbal expression of that inner life and the full range of feelings that
accompany it, then it becomes burdensome for him. He can
act out anger and frustration inside the family, it's true. But
ask him to express his sadness, his fear, his dependency—all
those feelings that would expose his vulnerability to himself
or to another—and he's likely to close down as if under some
compulsion to protect himself.

All requests for such intimacy are difficult for a man, but
they become especially complex and troublesome in relations with women. It's another of those paradoxes. For, to the
degree that it's possible for him to be emotionally open with
anyone, it is with a woman—a tribute to the power of the
childhood experience with mother. Yet it's that same early
experience and his need to repress it that raises his ambiva-

lence and generates his resistance.

He moves close, wanting to share some part of himself with her, trying to do so, perhaps even yearning to experience again the bliss of the infant's connection with a woman. She responds, woman style—wanting to touch him just a little more deeply, to know what he's thinking, feeling, fearing, wanting. And the fear closes in—the fear of finding himself again in the grip of a powerful woman, of allowing her admittance only to be betrayed and abandoned once again, of being overwhelmed by denied desires.

So he withdraws.

It's not in consciousness that all this goes on. He knows, of course, that he's distinctly uncomfortable when pressed by a woman for more intimacy in the relationship, but he doesn't know why. And, very often, his behavior doesn't please him any more than it pleases her. But he can't seem to help it.

That's his side of the ambivalence that leads to the approach-avoidance dance we see so often in relations between men and women.* What about her side?

On the surface, she seems to have little problem in dealing with closeness in a relationship. She's the one who keeps calling for more intimacy, who complains that he doesn't share himself fully enough, doesn't tell her what he's thinking and feeling. And while there's a partial truth in this imagery, the reality is more complex. Thus, when, as is sometimes the case, a woman meets a man who seems capa-

---

*Given the recent struggle to loosen traditional definitions of masculinity and femininity, we might assume that there would be differences in the intimate relations of men who are twenty-five and those who are fifty. And, although the younger men are likely to be more openly concerned with these issues, all the research evidence—my own and others'—suggests that integrating that concern into their behavior has been met with difficulties which, while usually not understood, parallel the issues I have been writing of here.

ble of the kind of intimacy she says she longs for, dreams about, we see that it's not just a matter of a woman who keeps asking for more in a relationship and a man who keeps protesting. Instead, we hear the other side of the story, as these words from a thirty-year-old patient show. Her blond curly head bent low, she sat in my office and wept bitterly:

> I can't figure out what's happening to me. I'm so anxious and churning inside I can't stand it. I try to read a book, and I find myself thinking of him. But it's not loving thoughts; it's critical, picky thoughts—anything negative, just to get me out of the relationship. Then, once I've convinced myself, I wonder: Why did I love him yesterday? And, if I did, how can it feel so miserable today? I get so confused I want to run and hide just to get away. But now I understand better what I'm scared of; I know it's my problem. I can't tolerate the intimacy, but I can't just break off the relationship like I used to and justify my escape by talking about his faults and inadequacies. But, at times, I actually feel myself being torn apart by this conflict going on inside me. [Tears streaming down her cheeks] How could it be such a burden to be loved?

It would be easy, and perhaps more comfortable, to write her off as some pathological case, a study in extremes that most of us have no reason to be concerned about. In fact, she's a woman in one of our most honored professions, a competent, highly functional person whose professional and personal life would seem to most of us the very model of accomplishment—good friends, a wide range of social and cultural activities, an active and committed work life. Altogether an intelligent, appealing, personable woman. The difference between her and so many others like her is only that, in the course of her therapy, she has learned to identify the cause of the anxiety that usually remains unrecognized, therefore, nameless and formless.

Most women know when a relationship makes them uncomfortable; they just have no idea why. They blame it on something particular about the person—he's too smart or not smart enough; he's too short or too tall; he's too passive or too aggressive; he's too successful or not successful enough; he's too needy or seems too self-contained. Some good reasons, some bad. Some true, some not. More to the point is how quickly a woman will rush for her checklist, how easily she will find ways to dismiss this person whose nearness is making her uneasy.

But even those women who are more able to tolerate closeness, who have fewer problems in sustaining a long-term relationship, are not without ambivalence about just how much of themselves they want to share, and when and how they want to do it. Trying to explain to me the one thing she thought most important in the success of her thirty-four-year marriage, one woman said almost casually, "It's worked so well because we both keep very busy and we don't see that much of each other." A sentiment she was not alone in expressing.

Surprisingly, women often have some sense—even if still an inchoate one—that their husbands' reticence about closeness serves their own needs as well. Thus, a twenty-nine-year-old woman responded to my questions about intimacy with some irritation.

> I can't stand all this talk about intimacy that's all around these days. Peter and I are plenty close—anyhow close enough to suit both of us, I guess. He's the strong, suffer-in-silence type. And maybe that's okay, I'm not sure anymore. Maybe I don't have the psyche for much more intimacy; maybe I couldn't tolerate any more than we have. There's something about the wall he builds around himself that's almost reassuring for me sometimes; I mean, like it's safe or something like that.

Even the fact that a husband is often less sensitive to what his wife is feeling than she might wish has both its positive side and its negative. On the one hand, a thirty-seven-year-old woman, married thirteen years, complains:

> I'm always genuinely interested in what's going on with him, and it's a problem for me—a pain, you know—that he never seems as interested in what's going on with me. I'd like him to want to know about me like I want to know about him.

On the other hand, she recognizes that there's a certain sense of relief for her in his not knowing or wanting to know—a reassurance that she can stay in control, that what's spoken and what isn't will be hers to choose. So, just minutes after she has voiced her complaint, she says thoughtfully:

> Talking about it this way makes me realize that it's not so simple as I'm saying. Actually, I have to admit that it's a double-edged thing. It's hard to explain, but sometimes I feel a real safe feeling in the fact that he doesn't notice what's happening with me. That way what I'm feeling and thinking is only up for notice and discussion if I bring it up. There's a way it feels safer even though there's also a kind of loneliness about it. It means it's all up to me to have it on the agenda. If I don't bring it up, forget it, Lloyd's certainly not going to. So, like I said, it works both ways; it's got its good points and bad ones. But one thing's sure, I can hide myself as much as I need to.

What is it she needs to feel safe from? Why is it she wants to hide? I asked the questions; she struggled for answers.

> I don't know exactly how to say it. It's not very clear, just a feeling. I mean, I know there are things he just wouldn't understand and it would only create a crisis. He gets very upset if I'm upset or depressed or something; it's like he can't stand it. He has trouble just listening without doing something, so he'll do or say something dumb like telling me I shouldn't feel bad. So then it ends up that I'm reassuring him and feeling ripped off, and like I got lost in the whole thing. It's too easy for me to lose myself and my thoughts. So why bother? It's better to go talk to a friend and get it off my chest that way than to try to deal with him.

Then there are the women who present the semblance of intimacy without much substance. We all know them—

women who seem to have an ineffable ability to attract people, who develop a kind of court around themselves. They
walk in an atmosphere that radiates warmth and openness,
that promises an intense and intimate closeness. But the husband of one such woman spoke bleakly about what it's like
to be married to her:

> Everybody gets a piece of the action but me. She looks like
> she's wonderful at closeness just so you don't get too close.
> She's got a million friends and they all think she's great. Ev-
> eryone comes to her for advice or to cry on her shoulder, and
> she loves it all. It makes her feel like the queen bee—always
> in the center of a swarm. But the truth is, she uses it to bind
> people to her, gets them to need her; that's the only way she
> feels secure. If someone catches on and wants something in
> return—I mean if they want something besides her big, loving
> mama number—they get run out of the court. I don't know
> exactly how she manages it, but she does, and it always turns
> out to be some problem with them, never with her. Now that
> the kids are grown, they're catching on, too. She's like mer-
> cury, she's so elusive; no one can get hold of her.

Surprised at the bitterness of the outburst from this
quiet, contained man, I commented, "Yet you've been married to her for twenty-three years. What keeps you here?"
With a small, sad smile, he replied:

> I guess the same thing that keeps others around—the seduc-
> tion. There's always the hope that she'll deliver what she pro-
> mises, and that if she ever does, it'll be worth the wait. Mean-
> while . . . well, I'm hooked, that's all; I keep going towards her,
> she keeps backing off. Oh, she'll be there if I want to cry my
> guts out—that's just what she wants from everybody. But try
> to get at her guts and you're in for trouble. All of a sudden that
> sweet, wonderful warmth can turn icy cold. [Pausing thought-
> fully for a moment, he backtracked] No, that's not right. On the
> outside, she manages to keep up the façade, and then some-
> how she turns things around as if you're the one who hurt her
> by asking for something impossible. But underneath there's
> ice.

What can we make of women like this? They excel in the social skills; they're artful at nurturance—both qualities for which they have been well schooled from girlhood on. But perhaps nurturance is not to be confused with intimacy.

I thought about this for a long time—about how to disentangle nurturance and intimacy, about whether it would make sense to do so. The issue began to puzzle me earlier when I looked at men whose ability to nurture was not in doubt but whose capacity for intimacy was. Of course I had noticed this in women before. But, since women are both the designated nurturers and the most articulate champions of intimacy in this society, the issue never came fully to the fore as a problem requiring explanation until I set out to understand men who nurture and their relationship to intimacy.

They're not a common lot, it's true, but they exist. I know them; I even live with one. And, as I struggled to make sense out of some of the issues that arose about men and intimacy, I kept asking myself, "Where do men who nurture fit? How can I explain the Allens, the Hanks, the Marks—few though they may be?" Friends with whom I talked of these problems when understanding still eluded me raised the same questions: "What about men who nurture? What about your own husband?"

I gave these pages to my husband to read, saying, "What about it? Am I being unfair to men in talking about their blocks to intimacy as I have?" We talked; we argued; we agreed; we disagreed. Thousands of words later, he finally said,

> I think you're right; what you've written is true about me, too. I keep trying to be more open and let you in on what goes on inside me, but it's damn hard. I know I've gotten better at it after twenty years of living with you, but it doesn't come easily and naturally. And lots of times I can't do it.

"But how do I make sense out of that when you're the most nurturing man I know," I lamented. To which he replied, laughing, "I don't know, but then I don't have to; it's your book."

Then we had a fight one day—a fight over the most classical of issues between men and women. I had asked him to do something to which I thought he had given assent. Actually, he had, as is his wont, said nothing. When, weeks later, the task was still not done, I asked again, only this time with some heat. "Stop pushing me," he said edgily. "I will if you'll answer me," I retorted. Then more quietly, "If you don't want to do it, why can't you just say so?" No answer. I waited a while. Finally, unable to tolerate the heavy silence, I said, "What's going on for you? What are you thinking?" "Nothing," came the surly reply. "How can you be thinking nothing?" I began to shout. "Christ, you never leave anything alone," he stormed as he left the room. And I, trailing after him, practically screamed, "It's because you never tell me what's going on in that head of yours so it could be finished." By then, both of us were standing in the hallway, and suddenly I was convulsed with laughter while he stared at me nonplused at this unexpected turnabout. "What's so funny," he growled. "We're right off the pages of my book," I gasped when I finally gained some control.

He talked then, his words coming with difficulty. "You ask me to do things and always assume that I know how. You don't ask me if I can, you just assume—as if I'm *supposed* to know all about those things. Then if I'm not sure how, it's hard to tell you that. So I think that I'll try to figure it out, then get it done. Meanwhile, I get busy and forget, then you remind me and I feel guilty, so I get defensive, and . . . well, what's to say?"

In amazement, I said to myself and to him, "And it took twenty years to tell me that? All these years when we'd have one of these exchanges, I thought you were being hostile.

And you were just *scared?* Why couldn't you tell me?" "I don't know, it's just hard," he said with difficulty. Then, smiling impishly, "But after reading your book, I'll be damned if I'll let you be *that* right about men." And, more seriously, "Besides, I'm learning."

It became clear to me then—not so much from anything in the content of our argument, but in its process. Nurturance is not intimacy. It may be connected to intimacy, may even sometimes be a result of it, but the two are distinct and separate phenomena. Nurturance is caretaking. Intimacy is some kind of reciprocal expression of feeling and thought, not out of fear or dependent need, but out of a wish to know another's inner life and to be able to share one's own. Nurturance can be used as a defense against intimacy in a relationship—a cover to confuse both self and other, to screen the fact that it doesn't exist. It can be used manipulatively—as a way to stay in control, as a way to bind another and ensure against the pain of loneliness.

We've all seen women who use their nurturant arts thus —binding children, husbands, friends to them through their generous, sometimes selfless, giving. But we don't think of men doing it. Yet it happens. A male friend, one who has thought deeply about his own nurturant tendencies, confessed:

> The kind of nurturance I offer to women makes them very dependent on me. After all, how many guys are good at caretaking or at listening? And, as a result, a woman will reveal her soul to me and will tell me she's never had such an intimate relationship. But the truth is that they're so seduced by my nurturant style that they don't notice that I'm pretty careful about revealing my own vulnerabilities. It all seems very benign, but I'm quite aware that it's one of the ways a man can retain power over a woman; he doesn't have to dominate her in any oppressive way, he can dominate by giving her so much that he ties her to him for as long as he wants. She becomes emotionally dependent, then he's safe.

A few men even talked about their capacity for sexual nurturance and the binding effect it has on a woman. It's not an easy subject to talk about, especially when facing a woman. But one thirty-six-year-old man in his second marriage spoke with particular eloquence:

> I don't want this to sound Machiavellian, but I developed all the arts of being a very good lover because they serve me well. I don't mean that I don't enjoy giving a woman pleasure—I do, very much. But I also know that it's one way to hook her, too. If you can open a woman up to a level of sexual passion she hasn't known before, she can become very dependent on you for that and you can have some assurance that she'll be around when you need her. [Somewhat uncomfortably] I hope you understand what I'm saying and that these words won't be used against me. I mean, I don't want to be portrayed as some sexist pig who uses women sexually; that's not the point I'm trying to make. I'm saying that I can only allow myself to be vulnerable when a woman is thoroughly hooked. I don't mean that I want to disempower her, but I'm scared that I can't hold her otherwise.

For both men and women, then, nurturance is a complex phenomenon that can have several meanings; for both, it can be a way of gaining love, of palliating fears of abandonment, of ensuring safety and security. None malevolent in themselves. But, however benign the motive, when a person nurtures out of fear and insecurity, it can also be a barrier to intimacy since it means that there's anxiety about revealing the "true" self for fear of losing the loved and desired one.

What all this says is that, despite the cant about women being available for intimacy and men being unavailable, they are both likely to experience problems and pressures in an intimate relationship. But, given the combination of the social roles for which they were trained and their early developmental experiences inside the family, what makes intimacy feel risky is different for each of them.

For a woman, the problem of finding and maintaining the boundary between self and a loved other is paramount. The continuity of identification with mother means that the tie is never quite severed—an invisible cord that fastens them to each other in a powerful bond that doesn't exist between mother and son.

A mother understands her son's differences from herself, indeed emphasizes them with pride and pleasure. That helps him in the task of separation. But there are no obvious differences to separate mother and daughter—no differences in their physiology, none in the requirements of the social role for which the girl child is destined. Thus, even when she conscientiously struggles against it, a mother looks at her daughter and sees there a miniature of herself—a reincarnation of her own past—just as a daughter sees her own future in her mother's present existence.

This fusion of identities and the struggle a girl engages to break those bonds foretells the future of her adult emotional relationships. "The basic feminine sense of self is connected to [others in] the world," writes Nancy Chodorow, "the basic masculine sense of self is separate."* Compared to a man, therefore, a woman remains more preoccupied with relational issues, gives herself more easily to emotional relationships, and reaches for attachment and emotional connection with an insistence and intensity that often startles her as well as the man in her life.

But this need for intimacy and connection is not without its paradoxical side. Because her boundaries can be so easily breached, she begins to fear that she's losing some part of herself—not just because someone is taking something from her but because, unless she's constantly vigilant, she's all too likely to give it away. For her, therefore, maintaining herself as a separate person in the context of an intimate relation-

*Chodorow, op. cit., p. 169.

ship is the dominant issue, the one she'll wrestle with from girlhood on.

A thirty-nine-year-old professional woman, married four years, spoke about just such fears. For her, they were so keenly felt that she had avoided intimate relationships with men until she met her husband five years ago. There were men in her life earlier, of course—even some relatively long-term relationships. But she fled from them in fear each time she began to feel, in her words, "too intensely"—not necessarily because of what a man might ask of her but because she was so frightened of her own internal responses.

> It took a long time before I could get married because I was so scared of getting that close to someone. I still worry because it's so easy to lose myself. I'm always afraid because I know I could sell myself out too easily and for a cheap price.

"What do you mean when you say you could 'sell yourself out'?" I asked.

> I mean that I can forget who I am and what I really need just to feel loved and taken care of and approved of. When John and I are having problems, I can't think about anything else; I can't do my work as competently as I feel I should—things like that. Then I feel like I'm disappearing, like maybe I'm just a product of someone's imagination.

"What happens when you begin to feel like that?" I wanted to know.

> [Laughing tensely] Oh boy, it's a mess. I get angry at John. I know it's a way to defend against him—or maybe it's more accurate to say it's the way I defend against what I might do to myself when I feel that isolated, I mean, what I might give away just not to feel that way.
>
> You know, men are different. I know John loves me, but no matter what's going on, it doesn't interfere with his work. Even when the baby is sick, or if our relationship would be in trouble, none of it interferes with his going to work and doing his job in a very single-minded way. I go, too, because I have

to. You know, you meet your responsibilities, no matter what. But my body's there; my mind and my heart are distracted. It's terribly upsetting to feel that way—not good at all for my self-esteem to crumble that way.

"And is there some patterned way you handle those feelings?" I asked.

You bet there is! I withdraw. Ask my husband, he'll tell you. It's like I put a steel wall around me. It's the way I protect myself from myself and that terrible passivity that can come over me where it feels like I've disappeared. I have to talk to myself and remind myself that there's a competent me, I mean the one who got through graduate school and all. [Sheepishly] With honors, too.

"Is that withdrawal a source of conflict between you and John?" I wondered.

Sometimes it is, of course. But I think what makes this marriage possible for me is that he seems to be able to let me do it without getting too upset. The fact is that he has his own troubles with closeness, so as long as the distant times and close ones are not so out of whack that we might not recognize each other, it's okay.

It's partly because of a woman's problems in maintaining the boundaries of self that friendships play such an important part in her life. Unlike most men, a woman understands the depth of her craving for emotional connection. But the rules that structure relations between men, women, and marriage and her own internal needs come together to make it difficult to retain the integrity of the self she has built with such effort. The norms of friendship, however, permit physical distance and psychological separation—indeed, at various times, require both for the maintenance of the relationship—thus providing the safety within which intimacy can occur without violation of self.

Parenthetically, it's the same with courtship—but not just for women. There, too, the structure of the relationship protects against the immediacy of the difficulties with intimacy. Whatever the level of intimacy and self-exposure, courting couples are not thrust into the kind of close, daily contact a marriage requires. There are acceptable ways of maintaining separation and distance, of protecting against vulnerability and intrusion. Before the marriage, too, expectations remain somewhat restrained; fears, feelings, needs generally are kept in check. What seems like a right after marriage is still considered a privilege in courtship. Whether in a legal marriage or not, when couples move from living separately to living together in a committed relationship, these issues of managing intimacy and expectation come to the surface—a shift that often comes so suddenly and unexpectedly after the marriage that it seems incomprehensible to the people involved.

How the conflicts are handled depends on the couple— on the ability of the individuals involved to tolerate both closeness and distance, to establish the boundaries of self while, at the same time, permitting a satisfactory level of emotional connection and attachment; in essence, on their capacity to move comfortably between separation and unity. But, however well or badly they are dealt with, these problems about which I have been writing will be there, requiring resolution. And they will be felt most keenly in any relationship that has the aura of permanence, that recreates the old family.

For men, who come to define themselves in terms of the denial of the original connection, the issue of unity is the most pressing. The problem that plagues their emotional relationships is their difficulty in allowing another to penetrate the boundaries sufficiently to establish the communion, the unity, that's necessary for a deep and sustained intimacy with another.

For women, it's the other way around. Because they come to define themselves by affirming that original connection, the problem of separation is in the forefront. Their more permeable boundaries and greater relational concerns make women less certain that they can maintain the hard-won separation, even that they want to maintain it. The possibility of merger with another, therefore, remains both a threat and a promise—a persistent strain in their relationships as they move ambivalently from the fear of violation and invasion to the hunger for that old symbiotic union.

Yet we all know women who seem not to have difficulties in close relationships—women who seem gladly to give themselves over to another, who apparently take their definition of self from that relationship without the conflict I'm speaking of here. It's another of those paradoxes that make this subject of women and men and their relationships with each other so endlessly fascinating. For this stereotypic image is both true and not true.

The truth is the simple one, as feminist writers have been telling us for almost two decades now. There are benefits in the connection to a man and, even in this so-called liberated age, few rewards for the woman who seeks to maintain an independent self. From earliest childhood, she has been socialized to derive her status from another—to know that she would grow up to marry a man through whom she would live vicariously. Even today, if a woman is married, she's still generally "placed" in the world according to who her husband is. And, if she has children, their successes or failures are taken to be hers. No surprise, then, that she so often seems to give herself to relationships so easily.

But such relationships are not necessarily intimate ones. And, when we look below the surface, a reality emerges that's more complex than we have heretofore understood. Then we find that women have their own problems in dealing with intimacy and build their own defenses against it—that, like their men, women also experience internal conflict about closeness which creates anxiety and ambivalence, if not outright fear. In relating to men, however, women rarely have to face the conflict inside themselves squarely, precisely because men take care of the problem for them by their own unmistakable difficulties with closeness and connection—because men tend to be so self-contained and protected from intrusion, except in the matter of sex. This, more than any other, is the area in which the conflicts of both—their differences and similarities—can be seen most clearly.

(5)

The Sexual Dilemma

WIFE: I say that foreplay begins in the morning.

HUSBAND: It seems to me being sexual would make us closer, but she says it works the other way—if she felt closer, there'd be more sex.

IT'S A COMMON COMPLAINT in marriages—wives and husbands all too often divided as these two are. We wonder about it, ask each other questions, try to persuade the other with reason, and, when that fails, we argue. Sooner or later we make up, telling each other that we'll change. And, in the moment the words are said, we mean them. We try, but somehow the promises aren't fulfilled; somehow, without thought or intention, we slip back into the old ways. The cycle starts again; the struggle is resumed.

We're told by the experts that the problem exists because we don't communicate properly. We must talk to each other, they insist—explain what we need and want, what feels good, what bad. So "communication" has become a household word, the buzzword of the age. We think about it, talk about it, read books, take courses, see therapists to learn how to do it. We come away from these endeavors with resolutions that promise we'll change our ways, that we'll work with our partner on being more open and more expressive about what we're thinking and feeling. But too often our good intentions come to naught, especially when it comes to reconciling our sexual differences.

These are difficult issues, not easily amenable to intervention by talk, no matter how earnest, how compelling our efforts at honesty may be. One couple, aged thirty-three and thirty-five, married eight years and the parents of two children, told of these differences. Speaking quickly and agitatedly, the wife said:

> Talk, talk, talk! He tries to convince me; I try to convince him. What's the use? It's not the words that are missing. I don't even know if the problem is that we don't understand each other. We understand, all right. But we don't like what we know; that's the problem.

Her husband's words came more slowly, tinged as they were with resignation and frustration.

> I understand what she wants. She wants us to be loving and close, then we can have sex. But it's not always possible that way. We're both busy; there are the kids. It can't be like a love affair all the time, and if we have to wait for that, well [his words trailing off] . . . what the hell, it'll be a long wait.

The wife, speaking more calmly but with her emotional turmoil still evident just below the surface of her words:

> He complains that I want it to be like a love affair, but that's not it. I want to feel some emotion from him; I want an emotional contact, not just a sexual one.

The husband, vexed and bewildered:

> When she starts talking about how I'm sexual but not emotional, that's it; that's where I get lost. Isn't sex emotional, for Christ's sake?

From both husband and wife, an angry yet plaintive cry. It's not words that divide them, however. They tell each other quite openly what they think, how they feel. It just doesn't seem to help in the ways they would wish. But, if it's not a simple matter of communication, then what is it that makes these issues seem so intransigent, so resistant to resolution even with the best intentions we can muster?

Some analysts of society point to the culture, to the ideologies that have defined the limits of male and female sexuality. Certainly there's truth in that. There's no gainsaying that, through the ages of Western society, women's sexuality has come under attack, that there have been sometimes extreme pressures to control and confine it—even to deny its existence. There's no doubt either that we have dealt with male sexuality with much more ambivalence. On the one hand, it too has been the object of efforts at containment; on the other, we have acknowledged its force and power—indeed, built myth and monument in homage to what we have taken to be its inherently uncontrollable nature.

Such social attitudes about male and female sexuality, and the behavioral ideals that have accompanied them, not only shape our sexual behavior but affect our experience of our own sexuality as well. For culture both clarifies and mystifies. A set of beliefs is at once a way of seeing the world more clearly while, at the same time, foreclosing an alternative vision. When it comes to sex—precisely because it's such a primitive, elemental force—all societies seek some control over it and, therefore, the mystification is greater than the clarification. Thus, for example, Victorian women often convinced themselves that they had no sexual feelings even when the messages their bodies sent would have told them otherwise if they had been able to listen. And, even now, men often engage in compulsive sexual behavior that brings them little, if any, pleasure without allowing themselves to notice the joylessness of it. Both behaviors a response to cultural mandates, both creating dissonance, if not outright conflict, when inner experience is at odds with behavioral expectations.

The blueprint to which our sexuality conforms, then, is drawn by the culture. But that's not yet the whole story. The dictates of any society are reinforced by its institutional arrangements and mediated by the personal experience of the people who must live within them. And it's in that confluence of social arrangement and psychological response that we'll come to understand the basis of the sexual differences that so often divide us from each other.

For a woman, there's no satisfactory sex without an emotional connection; for a man, the two are more easily separable. For her, the connection generally must precede the sexual encounter:

> For me to be excited about making love, I have to feel close to him—like we're sharing something, not just living together.

For him, emotional closeness can be born of the sexual contact.

> It's the one subject we never get anywhere on. It's a lot easier for me to tell her what she wants to hear when I feel close, and that's when I get closest—when we're making love. It's kind of hard to explain it, but [trying to find the words] . . . well, it's when the emotions come roaring up.

The issues that divide them around intimacy in the relationship are nowhere to be seen more clearly than here. When she speaks of connection, she usually means intimacy that's born of some verbal expression, some sharing of thought and feeling:

> I want to know what he's thinking—you know, what's going on inside him—before we jump into bed.

For him, it's enough that they're in the same room.

> To me, it feels like there's a nice bond when we're together— just reading the paper or watching the tube or something like that. Then, when we go to bed, that's not enough for her.

The problem, then, is not *how* we talk to each other but *whether* we do so. And it's connected to what words and the verbal expression of emotion mean to us, how sex and emotion come together for each of us, and the fact that we experience the balance between the two so differently—all of which takes us again to the separation and individuation experiences of childhood.

For both boys and girls, the earliest attachment and the identification that grows from it are much larger, deeper, and more all-embracing than anything we, who have successfully buried that primitive past in our unconscious, can easily grasp. Their root is pure eros—that vital, life-giving force with which all attachment begins. The infant bathes in it. But we are a society of people who have learned to look on eros with apprehension, if not outright fear. For us, it is associated with passion, with sex, with forces that threaten to be out of our control. And we teach our young very early, and in ways too numerous to count, about the need to limit the erotic, about our fears that eros imperils civilization.

In the beginning, it's the same for children of either sex. As the child grows past the early symbiotic union with mother, as the boundaries of self begin to develop, the social norms about sexuality begin to make themselves felt. In conformity with those norms, the erotic and emotional are split one from the other, and the erotic takes on a more specifically sexual meaning.

But here the developmental similarities end. For a boy at this stage, it's the emotional component of the attachment to mother that comes under attack as he seeks to repress his identification with her. The erotic—or sexualized—aspect of the attachment is left undisturbed, at least in heterosexual men. To be sure, the incest taboo assures that future sexual *behavior* will take place with a woman other than mother. But the issue here is not behavior but the emotional structure that underlies it.

For a girl, the developmental requirement is exactly the opposite. For her, it's the erotic component of the attachment to a woman that must be denied and shifted later to a man;

the larger emotional involvement and the identification re-main intact.

This split between the emotional and the erotic compo-nents of attachment in childhood has deep and lasting sig-nificance for the ways in which we respond to relationships —sexual and otherwise—in adulthood. For it means that, for men, the erotic aspect of any relationship remains forever the most compelling, while, for women, the emotional com-ponent will always be the more salient. It's here that we can come to understand the depth of women's emotional connec-tion to each other—the reasons why nonsexual friendships between women remain so central in their lives, so impor-tant to their sense of themselves and to their well-being. And it's here also that we can see why nonsexual relationships hold such little emotional charge for men.

It's not, as folklore has held, that a woman's sexual re-sponse is more muted than a man's, or that she doesn't need or desire sexual release the way a man does. But, because it's the erotic aspect of her earliest attachment that has to be repressed in childhood if a girl is later to form a sexual bond with a man, the explicitly sexual retains little *independent* status in her inner life. A man may lust after *women,* but a woman lusts after *a man.* For a woman, sex usually has meaning only in a relational context—perhaps a clue to why so many girls never or rarely masturbate in adolescence or early adulthood.

We might argue that the social proscriptions against masturbation alone could account for its insignificance in girls and young women. But boys, too, hear exhortations against masturbation—indeed, even today, many still are told tales of the horrors that will befall them. Yet, except to encourage guilt and secrecy, such injunctions haven't made much difference in its incidence among them.

It would be reasonable to assume that this is a response to the mixed message this society sends to men about their sexuality. On the one hand, they're expected to exercise restraint; on the other, there's an implicit understanding that we can't really count on them to do so—that, at base, male sexuality cannot be controlled, that, after all, boys will be boys.

Surely such differences in the ways in which male and female sexuality are viewed could account for some of the differences between the sexes in their patterns and incidence of masturbation. But I believe there's something else that makes the social prohibitions take so well with women. For with them, an emotional connection in a relationship generally is a stimulus, if not a precondition, for the erotic.

If women depend on the emotional attachment to call up the sexual, men rely on the sexual to spark the emotional, as these words from a forty-one-year-old man, married fourteen years, show:

> Having sex with her makes me feel much closer so it makes it easier to bridge the emotional gap, so to speak. It's like the physical sex opens up another door, and things and feelings can get expressed that I couldn't before.

For women, emotional attachments without sex are maintained with little difficulty or discomfort; for men, they're much more problematic. It's not that they don't exist at all, but that they're less common and fraught with many more difficulties and reservations.

This is the split that may help to explain why men tend to be fearful of homosexuality in a way that women are not. I don't mean by this that women welcome homosexual stirrings any more than men do. But, for women, the emotional and the erotic are separated in such a way that they can be intensely connected emotionally without fear that this will lead to a sexual connection. For men, where the emotional connection so often depends on a sexual one, a close emotional relationship with another man usually is experienced as a threat.

We can see most clearly how deep these differences run when we compare the sexual behaviors of lesbians and homosexual men. Here, the relationships are not muddied by traditional gender differences, suspicions, and antagonisms, and the differences between men and women are stark—there for anyone to see.

In a series of intensive interviews with gay women and men, I was struck repeatedly by the men's ability to take pleasure in a kind of anonymous sex that I rarely, if ever, saw in the lesbian world. For gay women, sex generally is in the context of a relationship—transient perhaps but, for however long it lasts, with genuine elements of relatedness. There are no "fucking buddies" whose names are irrelevant or unknown among lesbians—a common phenomenon with homosexual men. The public bathhouses so popular with many gay men are practically nonexistent for the women because the kind of impersonal, fleeting sexual encounters such places specialize in hold no attraction for most of them.

Among gay men, a friendship that doesn't include sex is rare. With gay women, it's different. Like their straight sisters, lesbians can have intensely intimate and satisfying relationships with each other without any sexual involvement. Certainly a nonsexual friendship will sometimes slide over into a sexual relationship. But, when it does, it's the emotional aspect of the entire relationship, not just the sexual, that's at center stage for the women.

Whether a person is straight or gay, the character of the split between sex and emotion is the same. But the way it's experienced generally is quite different depending upon whether the sexual partner is a woman or a man. Among straight men, because the sexual involvement is with a woman, it calls up the memory of the infantile attachment to mother along with the old ambivalence about separation and unity, about emotional connection and separateness. It's likely, therefore, that it will elicit an intense emotional response—a response that's threatening even while it's gratifying. It's what men look for in their sexual relations with a woman, as these words from a thirty-four-year-old husband tell:

> It's the one time when I can really let go. I guess that's why sex is so important to me. It's the ultimate release; it's the one place where I can get free of the chains inside me.

And it's also what they fear. For it threatens their defenses against the return of those long-repressed feelings for that other woman—that first connection in their lives. So they hold on to the separation between the sexual and emotional, and thereby keep the repression safe. Thus, moments after speaking of sex as the "one place" where he could feel free, the same man spoke of his apprehensions:

> Much as I look for it, sex can also be a problem for me sometimes. I can get awfully anxious and tense about it. If I don't watch it, so much begins to happen that I get scared, like I don't know where I'm at. So that puts a damper on things. I'm a little ashamed to say it, but I can do a whole lot better sexually with someone else—you know, someone I don't care about —than I can with her. With someone like that, it doesn't mess up my insides and get all that stuff boiling around.

"What is this 'stuff' that upsets you so?" I wondered aloud. Discomfited, he lowered his head and muttered, "I don't really know." "Could you try to figure it out for me?" I prodded gently.

> Well, it's really hard to put it into words, but let's see. The closest I can get is to say it feels like something I don't want to know about—maybe something I'm not supposed to know about. [A thoughtful pause] Jesus, I said that, but I'm not even sure what it means. Let's see! It's something like this. If I let it all happen—I mean, let all those feelings just happen—I don't know where it'll end. It's like a person could get caught

in them, trapped, so that you could never get out. Hell, I don't know. I've heard people say sex is like going back to the womb. Maybe that's it. Only you came out of the womb, and here it feels like you might never get out again. Does that make any sense to you?

Without doubt the sex act evokes a set of complex and contradictory emotional responses for both women and men —responses that leave them each feeling at once powerful and vulnerable, albeit in different ways. For a man, there's power in claiming a woman's body—a connection with his maleness that makes him feel alive, masterful, strong. A thirty-three-year-old man, married eight years, said wistfully:

> When things are quiet between us sexually, as they are now, it's not just the sex I miss, it's the contact.

"Do you mean the contact with Marianne?" I asked.

> Yeah, but it's what it stands for; it's not just her. I mean, it's the contact with her, sure, but it's how it makes me feel. I guess the best word for that is "alive"; it makes me feel alive and [searching for the word] I guess you could say, potent.

At the same time, there's anxiety about the intense, out-of-control feelings that are moving inside him—feelings that leave him vulnerable again to the will and whim of a woman.

> I'm not always comfortable with my own sexuality because I can feel very vulnerable when I'm making love. It's a bit crazy, I suppose, because in sex is when I'm experiencing the essence of my manhood and also when I can feel the most frightened about it—like I'm not my own man, or I could lose myself, or something like that.

It deserves a slight detour to comment on the phrase "the essence of my manhood," used by this man to describe his sexual potency and feelings. It makes intuitive sense to us;

we know just what he means. Yet it set me to wondering: What is the essence of womanhood?

Some women, I suppose, might say it lies in nurturance, some might speak about mothering, most probably would be puzzled because there would be no single, simple answer that would satisfy. But one thing is sure: For most women, the "essence of womanhood" would not lie in their genitals or in their experience of their sexual powers. That it's such a common experience among men is, perhaps, an effect of their early difficulties in establishing a male identity. Nothing, after all, more clearly separates a boy from his mother than this tangible evidence of his maleness.

This aside now done, let's return to the complex of feelings a man experiences around a sexual connection with a woman. There's comfort in being in a woman's arms—the comfort of surrender to the feelings of safety and security that once were felt so deeply, the warming sense of being nurtured and nourished there once again. And there are enchantment and ecstasy to be found there as well—the thrill of experiencing the "essence of manhood," the delight of recapturing the unity with another that had to be forsworn so long ago. But it's also those same feelings that can be felt as a threat. For they constitute an assault on the boundaries between self and other he erected so long ago. And they threaten his manliness, as this culture defines it, when he experiences once again his own dependent needs and wishes.

Thus delight and fear play catch with each other—both evident in the words men use to describe the feelings and fantasies that sex elicits. They speak sometimes of "falling into a dark cavern," and at other times of "being taken into a warm, safe place." They say they're afraid of "being drawn into an abyss," and also that it feels like "wandering in a soft, warm valley." They talk about feeling as if they're drowning, and say also that it's like "swimming in warmth and sunshine." They worry about "being trapped," and exult about feeling "free enough to fly."

Sometimes the same man will describe his feelings with such contradictory words:

> It depends. Sometimes I can get scared. I don't even know exactly why, but I feel very vulnerable, like I'm too wide open. Then it feels dangerous. Other times, no sweat, it's just all pure pleasure.

Sometimes it's different men who speak such widely disparate thoughts. No matter. All together they tell us much about the intensity of the experience, of the pleasure and the pain that are part of the sexual connection.

For a woman, there's a similar mix of feelings of power, vulnerability, and pleasure. There's power in her ability to turn this man who usually is so controlled, so in charge, into what one woman called "a great big explosion" and another characterized as "a soft jellyfish." A thirty-four-year-old woman, married eleven years, put it this way:

> There's that moment in sex when I know I'm in control, that he really couldn't stop anymore because his drive is so great, that I feel wonderful. I feel like the most powerful person in that instant. It's hard to explain in words what that feels like —I mean, the knowledge I have at that second of my own sexual power.

And, alongside this sense of her own power, there's vulnerability also. Thus, sighing in bemusement at the intricacies of her own feelings, she continued:

> But it's funny because there's also that instant when he's about to enter me when I get this tiny flash of fear. It comes and goes in a second, but it's almost always there. It's a kind of inner tensing up. There's a second when instead of opening up my body, I want to close it tight. I guess it's like being invaded, and I want to protect myself against it for that instant. Then he's in and it's gone, and I can get lost in the sexual excitement.

The fear that each of them experiences is an archaic one —the remnants of the separation-unity conflict of childhood that's brought to the surface again at the moment of sexual union. The response is patterned and predictable. He fears engulfment; she fears invasion. Their emotional history combines with cultural mandates about femininity and masculinity to prepare them each for their own side; their physiology does the rest.

For men, the repression of their first identification and the muting of *emotional* attachment that goes with it fit neatly with cultural proscriptions about manliness that require them to abjure the emotional side of life in favor of the rational. Sex, therefore, becomes the one arena where it is legitimate for men to contact their deeper feeling states and to express them. Indeed, all too often, the sex act carries most of the burden of emotional expression for men—a reality of their lives that may explain the urgency with which men so often approach sex. For, if sex is the main conduit through which inhibited emotions are animated, expressed, and experienced, then that imperative and compulsive quality that seems such a puzzle becomes understandable.

But the act of entry itself stirs old conflictual desires that must be contained. This is the moment a man hungers for, while it's also the instant of his greatest vulnerability. As a woman takes him into her body, there are both ecstasy and fear—the ecstasy of union with a woman once again; the fear of being engulfed by her, of somehow losing a part of himself that he's struggled to maintain through the years.

For a woman, the repression of her first *erotic* attachment is also a good fit with the cultural proscriptions against the free expression of her sexuality. But, in childhood, there was no need to make any assault on her first identification with mother and the deep emotional attachment that lay beneath it; no need, either, to differentiate herself as fully and firmly as was necessary for a male child. In adulthood, therefore, she remains concerned with the fluidity of her boundaries, on guard against their permeability—a concern that's activated most fully at the moment of penetration.

This is one of those moments in life when the distinction between fantasy and reality is blurred by the fact that the two actually look so much alike. With entry, her boundaries have been violated, her body invaded. It's just this that may explain why a woman so often avoids the sexual encounter —a common complaint in marriages—even when she will also admit to finding it pleasurable and gratifying once she gets involved. For there are both pleasure and pain—the pleasure of experiencing the union, the pain of the intrusion that violates her sometimes precarious sense of her own separateness. Together, these conflicting feelings often create an inertia about sex—not about an emotional connection but about a sexual one—especially when she doesn't feel as if there's enough emotional pay-off in it to make it worth the effort to overcome her resistance to stirring up the conflict again.

This conflict can be seen in its most unvarnished form in the early stages of relations between lesbians. There's a special kind of ecstasy in their sexual relationship just because it's with a woman—because in a woman's arms the boundaries of separateness fall, the dream of a return to the old symbiosis with mother is fulfilled. But the rapture can be short-lived, for the wish for symbiosis belongs to the infant, not the adult. Once achieved, therefore, ecstasy can give way to fear—fear of the loss of self, which is heightened beyond anything known in the sexual bond with a man.

There's anxiety about boundaries in heterosexual sex, of course. But there's also some measure of safety that exists in this union with one's opposite. For, although sex between a man and a woman can be an intensely intimate experience, there's a limit, a boundary between them that can't be crossed simply by virtue of the fact that they're woman and man. It may, indeed, be one of the aspects of sex with a man that a woman finds so seductive—the ability to satisfy sexual need while still retaining the integrity of a separate sense of self. For, in heterosexual sex, the very physical differences help to reassure us of our separateness while, at the same time, permitting a connection with another that's possible in no other act in human life.

Between two women—just as there was with mother— there's likeness, not difference. Lesbians speak often of the pleasure in this identity, telling of their feeling that loving each other is akin to loving self. But this very identity also raises all the old issues of fusion with a woman and sets the stage for the ambivalent oscillation between desire and fear. This is the central conflict in the early stages of a lesbian relationship—the conflict which it must survive if it is to become a lasting one. And it's in their ability to surmount the conflicts these boundary issues produce while, at the same time, maintaining an extraordinary level of intimacy that enduring lesbian relationships may be most instructive for the heterosexual world.

But what about sexual relations between men? Where does male homosexuality fit into this picture? It's different, of course, as these matters of relationship and emotion differ between men and women.

First of all, the boundary problems are not so central for men as for women because, as we have seen, a man develops boundaries that are more rigid and inflexible than a woman's. Therefore, the threat of merger that inheres in the identity between two women will not be a serious issue for men. Rather, the central problem between men is more likely to be related to their difficulty in bridging the distance between them, not in how to maintain it. In fact, to the degree that their boundaries can be penetrated, the threat more likely comes in relations with a woman rather than with a man just because this is the connection that has been the denied one.

Second, because the split between the sexual and the emotional is such a dominant characteristic of male sexuality, relations with men relieve the pressure for an emotional connection that's always present in any interaction with a woman—whether sexual or not. It's this split that permits the kind of impersonal sex so common among homosexual men—sex that's erotically stimulating and exciting yet leaves the emotions relatively untouched; "high sensation, low emotion sex" is the way a male colleague characterized it. And it's this split that, at least until now, has made lasting emotional connections between homosexual men so much less common than among lesbians. When men relate to women, they must confront that split, try to heal it, if their relations are to survive. But, without women in their lives to insist upon the primacy of the emotional connection, it will often get attenuated, if not lost.

As I write these pages, some questions begin to form in my mind. "Is all this," I wonder, "just another way of saying that women are less sexual than men? What about the women we see all around us today who seem to be as easy with their sexuality as men are, and as emotionally detached?"

Without doubt there are today—perhaps always have been—some women for whom sex and emotion are clearly split. But, when we look beneath the behavior of even the most sexually active woman, most of the time we'll see that it's not just sex that engages her. It's true that such a woman no longer needs to convince herself that she's in love in order to have a sexual relationship with a man. But the key word here is *relationship*—limited, yes, perhaps existing only in a transitory fantasy, but there for her as a reality. And, more often than not, such relationships, even when they are little more than fleeting ones, have meanings other than sexual for a woman. For the sexual stimulus usually is connected to some emotional attachment, however limited it may be. And what, at first glance, might seem simply to be a sexual engagement is, in reality, a search for something else.

We need only listen to women to hear them corroborate what I'm saying here. When asked what it is they get in their more casual sexual encounters, even those who consider themselves the most sexually liberated will generally admit that they're often not orgasmic in such transient relationships. "When I was single, I'd sleep with someone who appealed to me right away, no problems," said a recently married twenty-seven-year-old breezily. "Did you usually have orgasms in those relationships?" I asked her. Laughing, she replied, "Nope, that was reserved." "Reserved for what?" I wanted to know. Saucily, "For the guy who deserved it." "And what does that mean?" Finally, she became serious. "I guess it means I have to trust a guy before I can come with him— like I have to know there's some way of touching him emotionally and that I can trust him enough to let him into that part of me."

"What's in it for you?" I asked all the women who spoke this way. "Why get involved at all if it's not sexually gratifying?" Without exception, they said they engaged sexually because it was the only way they could get the other things they need from a man. "What things?" I wanted to know. The answer: Something that told of their need for relationship and attachment rather than sex. They spoke of wanting "hugging more than fucking," of how it "feels good to be connected for a little while." They talked almost urgently of the "need to be held," "to feel needed by someone," of how important it is that "there's someone to give something to and take something from."

It's true, men also will speak of the need to be held and hugged. But orgasm generally is not in question and hugging is seldom an end to be desired in and for itself. In fact, it's one of the most common complaints of women that, even in the context of a stable relationship, such tender physical contact becomes too quickly transformed into a prelude to sex. "Why can't he just be happy to hold me; why does it always have to lead to fucking?" a woman complains. "I hold her and we hug and cuddle; I like it and I like her to hold me, too. But there's a natural progression, isn't there?" her husband asks, mystified.

Whether in my research or in my clinical work, I hear the same story told—women who are sexually very active yet who only become orgasmic in the context of a relationship with a man they can trust, as these words illustrate. She's a forty-three-year-old woman in a four-year second marriage after having been single for seven years. Talking about some of the experiences of those years as a divorcée, she said:

> There wasn't any dearth of men in my life most of the time, and I learned a lot about myself and how I relate to them during those years. I found out that going to bed with someone was one thing, but getting satisfied sexually was another.
>
> When I got married the first time, I was practically virginal—hardly any experience with anyone but my husband. So I didn't know much about my own sexuality. I mean, I knew I was a very sexual woman, but I thought having orgasms was practically automatic, you know, just a matter of pushing the right buttons, so to speak. What a surprise when I got divorced and started sleeping around with a lot of guys! [With a rueful grin] All of a sudden it seemed like my body had a mind of its own and I just couldn't make it; I couldn't come, I mean. I'd get all hot and excited and . . . poof, nothing. I couldn't understand it; I mean, I had no idea what was happening.
>
> Then I got involved with a guy I really liked. It was an honest-to-God relationship with a good man who cared about me as a person, and lo and behold, I was orgasmic again. I didn't get it right away, but after a while, even if you're a dimwit, you get the point.

The flow of words stopped, as if she considered the "point" self-evident. Not certain just what she meant, I asked for an explanation. "What was it you finally 'got'?"

Well, after a couple of those experiences, I began to realize that something in me would withhold having an orgasm when I was with a man I didn't trust. I didn't plan it that way; it just happened. It didn't make any difference how attracted I was to him or how turned on I was, if I didn't trust him in some deep place inside me, then I wouldn't be able to come, and that was that.

Trust is, of course, an issue for men as well. Like the inorgasmic woman, a man, too, can become impotent in a sexual encounter with a woman he fears is untrustworthy. In recent years, we have heard more about such men than ever before—perhaps because there are more of them, perhaps only because these issues are more likely to be part of a public discussion these days. But, whatever their number, it's a much less common phenomenon than it is among women. Moreover, when impotence does hit, it's almost as likely to happen in the context of an emotional relationship as it is with a stranger. A thirty-one-year-old cook, married only a short time, spoke of both these moments when experience has taught him that impotency could become an issue for him:

It's a damned funny business and I can't know exactly when it'll happen. I finally figured out it happens when something scares me—you know, when I figure maybe it's not safe. [Looking perplexed] Sounds a little nuts, doesn't it? What's not safe? I don't know. Sometimes it would be when I was trying to get it on with someone I didn't know—like the first time with a woman. But that's from my past life—[laughing] I mean when I was single. It happens sometimes with LuAnn, too—not a lot, just sometimes. She's great—never makes me feel like I let her down or anything. But it worries me when it happens anyhow. Thing is, I don't really know why, but I think it's the same scared feeling, like something inside me goes, "Uh, oh—better watch out."

"Watch out for what?" I asked. He stood up, paced the room, tried to answer.

That's the thing; it's hard to put it in words. It's just "better watch out." With some person I don't know, I can figure I don't trust her so much so I get scared. After all, when you're at the peak in sex, you're damned vulnerable—right out there with everything hanging out, so to speak. [With a rush] I mean you're there, man! [Stopping then, as if hearing his own words for the first time, then continuing more calmly] Christ, I guess it's the same with LuAnn, isn't it? It's such an intense experience, sex, that you can't help exposing a lot, so sometimes you can't be sure you can trust *any* woman with it.

Obviously, most men as well as women prefer sex in the context of a relationship with a person to whom they have some emotional attachment. But, in contrast to women, for men, most of the time it's just that—a preference that can be put aside when, for whatever reasons, it cannot be honored. The fullness of the emotional experience may be diminished under conditions that are less than ideal for them, but their sexual pleasure and capacity for orgasm generally are not.

Indeed, for some men, sex is easier, less riddled with conflict, when it comes without emotional attachment. For there are still many men who suffer the madonna-whore split inside themselves—men who love the "good" woman but who lust after the "bad" one, men who can experience their sexuality fully only with a woman with whom there is no emotional connection. A thirty-eight-year-old accountant, married two years after having been divorced and single for six, said painfully:

I love Caroline but, damnit, sex just isn't as exciting anymore. I was a regular stud when I was single—always ready, yeah, at your service ma'am, no problems. [Turning to stare out the window which framed a lovely garden] Now it's all changed and I worry like hell about what it's going to do to our marriage. She's patient, but she admits she'd like more sex. But I seem to have lost interest. I go along for a while thinking sex just doesn't matter much to me anymore. Then some woman catches my attention and I feel the flash inside me that says, "Boy would I like to get my hands on *that.*" [Bewildered] I don't know! It was the same thing in my first marriage. I'd get it on with women I didn't give a damn about and fly high with it, but with my wife [his words trailing off] . . . I'm scared; I don't want it to happen again. [Retreating suddenly from the obvious emotion in the room, he laughed] What do you think? Do I need a shrink? Am I hiding some deep, dark secret about wanting to fuck my mother? Huh? What about it?

His thirty-one-year-old wife tells her side:

At the beginning, it was wonderful. I'm sexually pretty free. I mean, I'm not some kind of—what'll I say?—some kind of wild woman, but I'm cool. I like sex and there's not much I wouldn't do sexually. And Randy loved it when we were going together—or at least I thought he did. He acted like it anyway. But not long after we got married, it all changed.

"Then you didn't live together before you got married?" I asked.

No, we were in two different cities—about five hundred miles apart. So we had weekends together, when we could manage it, and one week's vacation. But we didn't go together very long before we got married. The five hundred miles seemed to get longer and longer, and in a few months we decided to stop fooling around and just do it. [Sighing as she remembered the past] They were wonderful months, though—especially in bed. It was like an explosion when we came together. And now . . . well, most of the time it's just kind of bloop and blah. I finally convinced him that we ought to try some therapy and we've been seeing someone for the last couple of months. But between you and me, I think he needs to do it alone. It's not like I think I'm perfect or anything, but I really think this is his problem, not mine. I keep having the feeling that now that we're married, he wishes I were a virgin or something. I know it sounds crazy, but that's what I feel.

"Has the couples therapy helped any? Has anything changed at all?" I wondered aloud.

Oh yeah, it's better—at least some of the time it is. But I get discouraged sometimes—and scared, too, I guess. It gets better for a while and I get all revved up and hopeful, then he just poops out again. And that's the way it is right now—up and down, up and down, over and over again.

And so it goes: "up and down, over and over again." We make some changes, and the old issues pop up again in new form. We move ahead, and something comes along to push us back. We think about it, wonder about it, fret about it, argue with each other, often forgetting that each step is a gain—a small one, perhaps, but a movement forward which, while it might not take us as far as we would wish, also doesn't permit an easy return to the old ways. Meanwhile, we continue to reach out to each other in yearning—searching for connection, for unity, for emotional release. And again we confront the central dilemma of our relations with each other. For the unity and connection that's at least momentarily possible in this union of two bodies—that makes sex so deeply satisfying—also touches our deepest and earliest fears.

(6)

Redefining Dependency

All are needed by each one; nothing is fair or good alone.

RALPH WALDO EMERSON

"INDEPENDENCE"—A WORD with sharply different meanings for men and for women. "Can you tell me," I asked, "what thoughts come immediately to mind when I say the word 'independence'?"

For men, it's almost universally something to be desired; for women, it's generally something to fear. Not one man I spoke with had any negative associations with the word, while most women did. By and large, men associate independence with such words as freedom, control, power, self-sufficiency, happiness. Women's thoughts turn to worries about being alone, not close to anyone, unnurtured. "It's kind of dangerous because it can get very lonely." "It means you won't get taken care of anymore." "It's risky business unless you're prepared to live alone."

Most women know in their heads that independence has some positive value as well, but in their hearts it's a notion that makes them uneasy at best, fearful at worst. Several women said the first word that came to their minds when they thought about "independence" was divorce. Others said it meant "nothing good" to them. The dominant theme, expressed in any number of ways, was: "Independence brings to mind tough ladies who are terribly lonely."

Even among the few women who spoke of independence positively, none gave it unqualifiedly high marks. A twenty-eight-year-old mother of one child who described independence as meaning "activity, strength, direction—all very positive out-there-in-the-world connections"—ended her comments by saying also, "and all very scary because it means you risk being a lonely old woman."

Men and women alike associate the word "strong" with the idea of independence. But the difference in their responses to that word, in what it means to them, is striking. For men, "strong" is an unconditional good—something to be sought, to be desired, to be prized—a quality to be owned with pride. For women, as with independence, strength also is a problem, suggesting both danger and isolation. "A strong, independent woman, that's like a red flag for people, especially men; they don't like it." Men think of strength as something that will keep them safe, the key to preserving autonomy. "If you're really strong and independent enough, you can feel safe." "Safe from what?" I asked. "From whatever or whoever might come along and try to run your life," was the answer. "If you want to protect your sovereignty, you'd better be strong enough to do it." An interesting word, "sovereignty"—one only a man would use in discussing such issues.

Although I had come to interview them about their marriages, and although we had talked for several hours before we turned to the subject of independence, rarely did a man think of the word only in the context of a relationship. Instead, it was for him a statement about himself in the world outside his marriage and family—a statement about the kind of person he was or wanted to be. Just the opposite for the women, whose remarks and associations almost always referred to a relationship—either one that existed in the present or one they hoped to have.

There are no surprises in any of this, nothing to require much discussion or explanation. Independence is a trait that's socially valued in men, not in women. Therefore, men think of it positively, women negatively. Who hasn't heard a man complain about some woman he knows who is "too independent"? Imagine anyone saying that about a man! The same is true of strength. Think about it! What imagery comes to mind with the words "He's a strong man"? What do we think when we hear "She's a strong woman"? Admiration for the man of strength. But what for the woman? At best, the response is an ambivalent one; at worst, it's hostile, often eliciting some derogatory remark about her lack of femininity.

Whatever the reasons, all this seems to affirm what we think we know: Women seek dependence; men, independence. But, as is true about so much in our relations with each other, things are not always what they seem.

"Let's pretend for a moment that something were to happen to your wife [or husband]," I said. "Would you want to marry again?"

Almost all the men answered with an unhesitating "yes." A few, those who had married very young and were still living in a long-term first marriage, said they wouldn't want to marry again for a while, that they would like to know what it was like to live alone. A fifty-two-year-old airplane mechanic, married thirty-two years, sighed wistfully:

> If there's any part of life I'd like to experience at this point, it's living alone as an adult.

But even this statement was modified a few sentences later.

> It might not last more than two months because the reality might be totally different from what I think it would be when there was nobody there to have those nice martinis waiting for me.

As he continued to think aloud with me, it became apparent that the "waiting martinis" were a metaphor for all the ways in which, experience has taught him, a woman in his life provides comfort, support, nurturance, and outright caretaking. And it became clear to him that his fantasy about living alone would, indeed, be short-lived.

> Well, I don't know. I got married in the first place because I thought it would make my life easier—I'd be able to pay more attention to what I was doing at work, you know, figure out what I was going to be doing instead of just drifting around. I wouldn't have to chase around for company; there'd be somebody taking care of things at home; you know, all that stuff. So how much different would I feel about all that now? Truth is, I'm not so sure; I mean, the work part's okay now, but the rest . . .

Some men qualified their answers by rephrasing the question to include the possibility of living with a woman without marriage. That done, they all envisioned a stable, in-house relationship. "What's the difference," I asked, "between marriage and a live-in relationship to which you're committed?" A relationship outside marriage, they agreed, implied a different level of commitment on their part—one in which they wouldn't feel so responsible financially, one from which they could withdraw more easily if it became disagreeable.

Interesting, isn't it, that the same men who speak of valuing independence so highly—who equate it with freedom, happiness, strength, and control—also say they would waste little time on the single life if something were to happen to their wives.

It's true that I was asking for a response to a fantasy, and that real life might bring a very different set of feelings, let alone behaviors. Still, the question evoked markedly different fantasies from women and men—differences which, irrespective of what the realities might be, were in themselves revealing.

Among the women, almost half said that they wouldn't marry again—many more among those who were living in long-term marriages than among those who had been married for less than ten years; many more also among those who had no children left in the home than among those who were still in the childrearing process. Some spoke hesitantly: "It's hard to say, of course, but I think I wouldn't want to be married again"; some unequivocally: "I've done that trip, no more marriage for me." However it was said, the message was clear: For some significant proportion of the women I met, marriage had at least as many costs as benefits.

A surprising response! Yet, on reflection, it makes sense. Women married a long time often begin to count the costs—feeling that the price for marriage has been the loss of parts of themselves they now want to recover.* Thus, they speak of wanting to "find out who I am by now"; of wishing to "see if I can retrieve the lost me." A forty-nine-year-old woman, married thirty years and struggling now to find a way to live the rest of her life productively, said:

> No, I don't think I'd marry again, at least not for a long while. I know I might be lonely, but I also know what marriage takes from a woman. And if I didn't get married, I might have a chance of finding myself again.

Of course, it's a lot easier for a woman to think such thoughts when the responsibilities of motherhood are behind her. It's at this time—especially when she sees her own daughter and others all around her in the first bloom of womanhood—that she often is freed to recall her own youth, to remember the young woman who managed life in the world outside the home so competently, the one who now feels like a stranger to her.

Some women were doubtful—uncertain about what they might want to do, afraid that in choosing to reclaim themselves they would be doomed to a lifetime of loneliness. "I'm

*Lillian B. Rubin, *Women of a Certain Age: The Midlife Search for Self* (New York: Harper/Colophon, 1981).

just not sure; it would be a hard decision." One woman who, at forty-one, recently completed a training course in stock-market analysis and is now at work at her first job since she married twenty-three years ago, snapped angrily:

> Damnit. Why are women the ones who have to make that choice? A man can be a whole person and still have a home and marriage and all the goodies that go with having a wife. But for us it's one or the other. It's not fair.

Yet, doubts or not, almost all said they would look forward to some time alone. Indeed, there was a wistfulness to be heard about the prospect because, as one thirty-six-year-old, who has followed her army husband around since their marriage eighteen years ago, said, "I wouldn't have to be giving away pieces of myself all the time."

Even among those women who were certain that they'd want to marry again as quickly as possible there was plenty of talk that suggested the terms of a new marriage would be quite different from the old, as these words spoken by a thirty-nine-year-old assistant bank manager tell:

> I'd never want to live alone if I could help it, so I'm sure I'd marry again—maybe not right away, but pretty quick, I think. But it wouldn't be the same as now, you can just bet. I've learned a lot these seventeen years, and we'd have a whole different agreement about how we'd live. No more Mrs. Goody Two-Shoes, always doing everything for everybody—not on your life.

What sense can we make of such seemingly contradictory declarations: Men who equate independence with freedom and happiness only to say moments later that they would marry again quickly if their wives were suddenly to be gone from their lives? And women who speak of independence with fear yet who, in imagination at least, seem so much less eager than their men to give it up were it to fall into their laps?

Such conflicting and inconsistent statements violate our expectations, our sense of order in the world, our beliefs about how women and men feel about their places in it. Yet it should not surprise us greatly to find once again that the cultural definitions of masculinity and femininity are not in harmony with the inner needs of the people who must live them out. For too long now, the economic independence of men has been mistaken for their emotional independence, while women's economic dependency has been taken to signify their emotional dependence as well. And women, at least, have long known that, despite the face they show to the world, their men often seem to them like children in want.

It's generally not a subject for public comment, but in the back regions of women's lives—when they're alone or with trusted women friends—the knowledge is shared. Their tone may be gentle: "He can be such a baby sometimes"; protective: "He hates me to see him hurt, so I pretend not to notice, and I'll just be extra nice at times like that"; loving: "He puts on this big, bad wolf act, but I know"; angry: "Men, they're so damned needy, only they won't ever admit it. It's all hidden under that self-reliant exterior, but puncture it and you see the real picture"; or sometimes mocking: "They hide behind this goddamn façade, and underneath there's a sniveling kid." However they're said, the words leave no doubt that women have at least some sense of the emotional vulnerability and dependency of their men.

In fact, men are both self-contained and needy. But the defenses they built long ago mask the need, and the structure of the society and the family within which they live out their lives supports the myth of their self-sufficiency.

The solace and protection of marriage, for example, are more readily available to a man than to a woman, especially after youth has passed. Like a fine wine, aging in a man is thought to add to his complexity and finesse; the "attractive older man" can make the heart of a twenty-year-old skip a beat. With a woman, it's quite another matter. Even in youth, she doesn't have the same social value as a man, isn't such a highly prized "commodity." As she ages, her situation worsens, so that by midlife her chances of finding a man with whom to share her life are slim indeed. Whatever a man's dependent needs are, therefore, they simply won't be as obvious as a woman's because there's usually a woman quickly and easily available to help obscure them.

Still, it is commonly understood by now that marriage benefits men in ways that women do not share. A man needs a wife to support his life in all the ways we know so well— to take care of all the irritating, distracting, time-consuming chores of daily life, from cooking the meals to getting the car fixed, from car-pooling the children to arranging the details of their joint social life. A man without a woman in his life can be overwhelmed when he confronts these tasks; a woman does them as a matter of course, almost as if they were second nature.

As I write these words, I think, "What about the men in families where such tasks are shared? Surely those men wouldn't be swamped by having to do them alone." And I wonder. For, even in families—growing in number but still comparatively few—where those tasks are attended to by both, it's a *sharing* of the responsibilities that we see, not one person attending to them all alone. And, in the still rarer situations where the roles are switched and the man becomes a househusband, neither the partners nor the social world in which they live takes what he does for granted. The wife is guiltily grateful—telling anyone who will listen how wonderful he is; the husband is gracefully generous while he wavers between feeling heroic and oppressed. But, whatever the emotional temper of the household and the people who live in it, househusbanding is almost always a temporary role for a man, and, while he does it, it's *never* as exclusively his as housewifery is for a woman.

All the research available shows that married men live longer, healthier lives than those who are single. The reverse is true for women; those who never marry live longer and with fewer physical or emotional problems than their married sisters. Widowhood may be difficult for both, but the life span of a woman is not affected by the death of her husband, even if she doesn't remarry. The same is not true for men, whose lives are in serious jeopardy if they do not marry again quickly.*

But, we might ask, can't we expect that the present generation of younger men will grow to be more self-sufficient about personal and household care than their fathers and grandfathers have been? And, since the problems that plague men who live alone are health related and often stem from inadequate care, wouldn't that change such statistics in the future? An interesting question to which there's no easy answer.

Certainly, if men become more capable of caring for their own physical needs, we might expect some changes in these statistics. But it's worth noticing that even these relatively obvious manifestations of men's dependency have, until quite recently, gone largely unheeded. For the ideology that insists that women are the dependent ones colors our perceptions so that we are blinded to the signals that would give us a different picture. Or, should we happen to notice that the reality contradicts our belief, we redefine dependence and independence to fit the ideology so that the ability of women to cope with the problems of daily life and to care for the needs of others as well as for themselves is not cred-

*Knud J. Helsing, Moyses Szklo and George W. Comstock, "Factors Associated with Mortality after Widowhood," *American Journal of Public Health,* Vol. 71 (1981), pp. 802–809; Mervyn Susser, "Widowhood: A Situational Life Stress or a Stressful Event?" *American Journal of Public Health,* Vol. 71 (1981), pp. 793–796. See also Jessie Bernard, *The Future of Marriage* (New York: Bantam Books, 1973).

ited to their independence or their capacity for autonomous living.

But, ideology aside, there's something else that's at stake for men in their relations with women—something that's more fundamentally important to their lives than the physical care they can usually count on, something for which they depend on women that, I believe, we have not yet understood. That something is related to the emotional side of life, which, as we are coming to understand more and more fully, is not unconnected to the fate of our bodies. And it's here that women fill a void for men. For, whether men are twenty-five or fifty-five, women usually are the emotional ballast for them—providing not just the stability they need but the place and the encouragement for emotional expression that is unavailable elsewhere in most men's lives. Nowhere do we see this more clearly than when we look at men and women and the patterns of their friendships.

I recently completed a series of interviews about friendship with over two hundred men and women—married, divorced, single—who ranged in age from twenty-five to fifty-five and came from all walks of life. The results of the research are unequivocal: Women have more friendships (as distinct from collegial relationships or workmates) than men, and the difference in the content and quality of their friendships is marked and unmistakable.

Over two-thirds of the single men couldn't name a best friend. Of those who could, it was much more likely to be a woman than a man who held that place in their lives. In contrast, over three-fourths of the single women had no problem in identifying a best friend, and almost always that person was a woman. Among those who were married, far more men than women named a spouse as a best friend, their most trusted confidante, and/or the one they would be most likely to turn to in emotional distress. For the married women, it was a strikingly different picture. Even when a woman did name her husband to one or more of these roles, it was never exclusively his, as was most likely to be the case with a man. Most women identified at least one, usually more, trusted friends to whom they could turn in a troubled moment, and they spoke openly and ardently about the importance of these relationships in their lives.

Generally, women's friendships with each other rest on shared intimacies, self-revelation, nurturance, and emotional support. In contrast, men's relationships are marked by shared activities. Talk usually centers around work, sports, sharing expertise—whether about how to fix a leak in the roof or which of the new wine releases is worthy of cellaring. And, of course, they trade complaints and concerns about women along with tales of exploits. But, most of the time, their interactions are emotionally contained and controlled—a good fit with the social requirements of manly behavior.

Thus, even when a man claimed a best friend, the two shared little about the interior of their lives and feelings. It wasn't unusual, for example, to hear a man say that he didn't know his friend's marriage was in serious trouble until he appeared one night asking if he could sleep on the couch. And men who claimed years of close friendship failed to confide their distress at the discovery of a wife's extramarital affair. They talked about the problems of women and men; they joked about sexual differences, about the difficulty in understanding "them." But it was an abstract discussion, held under cover of an intellectual search for understanding rather than a revelation of the content of their lives and feelings. They didn't say to each other, "I feel lonely even though I'm married. What can I do about that?" "I feel hungry for sex and my wife isn't available."

When asked to explain their failure to speak of more personal matters with their friends, some men were quick to acknowledge that they couldn't share the pain they felt, couldn't risk allowing another man to see the vulnerability. Others, however, credited an inbred sense of privacy, a deep-seated belief that marriage requires that kind of loyalty. Good reasons—reasons to be honored. But those same men also acknowledged that they didn't talk to friends about the fears and conflicts inside them that have nothing to do with anyone else—about their disappointments in themselves, about their fear of failure, about the difficulty of always having to put on a show of strength and independence.

Validating the results of my own research, *Newsweek* magazine recently published an article about this paucity of close and nurturing relations among men in which the writer commented with sadness and envy, "I've always been amazed at the nurturing emotional support that my wife can seek and return with her close female friends. Often the most intimate and intense problems are shared and therefore diminished through empathy. Her three-hour talks with friends refresh and renew her far more than my three-mile jogs restore me. In our society it seems as if you've got to have a bosom to be a buddy. . . . Granted the women's movement has made great strides in convincing men that vulnerability is nothing to be ashamed of but is instead a badge of humanity. Suddenly, to be male and vulnerable is to be utterly acceptable—but only to women. . . . Let one male approach another with talk of needing a kindred spirit and the listener will start looking for the closet from which the speaker must have emerged."*

A sad commentary. But oddly enough it represents progress also. Fifteen years ago, we hadn't yet begun to know there was a problem here, hadn't yet found the thoughts or the words with which to give it expression. Today, the sub-

*Elliot Engel, "Of Male Bondage," *Newsweek,* Vol. 99 (June 21, 1982), p. 13.

ject of men and their problems in intimate relationships merits a serious commentary in a major national magazine whose pages usually are devoted to issues of the world that we consider the large and important ones. Talking about such problems, even understanding how we come to share them, doesn't guarantee change, of course. This we have found out all too forcefully in these years. But without talk, without understanding, we are also without hope. For change comes in small steps—starting first with the realization that a problem exists.

In my friendship study, I found a few men who talked about their difficulty in developing friendships with other men, who acknowledged the competitiveness that's built into male relationships and spoke of their wish to change it. But, on issues as deep-seated as these, transforming wish into reality can be very hard. Therefore, most men sat silently for a long while when I asked, "Who would you turn to if you came home one night and your wife announced she was leaving you?" When they finally spoke, it was with great hesitation as the realization came to them that there would be no friend to whom they could turn in that moment of pain and shock.

Some men thought of family—a sister, a mother, much more seldom a brother. One thirty-year-old California man who had insisted that he had "twenty intimate friends I can go to for just about anything" said he would call his mother in Michigan. When I asked, "What about all these friends you've talked about; wouldn't you go to even one of them?" He replied quickly, "Sure, sure I would. But first I'd have to put myself together, you know, get over the first shock so I wouldn't just be falling apart."

Small wonder, then, that women speak so often about being the singular source of emotional support in the lives of their men. Small wonder, too, that so many women claim that the emotional vitality in the relationship comes from them—some even commenting about how they make their men feel alive. "Without me, everything would be so damned bland around here it would be like he was dead," grumbled one woman. "He feeds on me," said another, not with hostility but simply as if expressing an elementary truth. "I don't know how much he understands it, but that's the real reason he needs me. I'm his tie to life, if you know what I mean."

Interestingly enough, it's a claim that many men don't dispute. Some will question themselves, understanding that there's something amiss in this way of relating to a woman even if they don't know what. Others will simply put a different cast on the issue, assuming that it's part of what a man expects from a woman, not some problem in themselves or of men in general that deserves attention.

It's another of those complicated issues. For, by furnishing this kind of emotional sustenance, a woman can tie a man to her—can give him the one thing she knows he cannot get for himself elsewhere. Housekeeping services can be bought; certain kinds of companionship can be had from another man; the emotional services usually can come only from a woman. But, at the same time, she may feel burdened by the weight of his need, by the fact that it falls upon her alone—as the conflict between this couple, married almost fifteen years, shows.

Seven years ago, when their two children were both in school full time, the wife—an attractive woman who looks much less than the thirty-five years she claims—set out to complete the college education that was aborted with her marriage. She works now as the assistant to the personnel manager in a manufacturing firm. It's essentially a good marriage, and much of the interview showed very little strain. But when it came to this issue of dependence and independence, she spoke with some asperity as she complained:

It's incredible, he's supposed to be the independent one, but he can't take time off from work if I'm not there with him. When I take vacation time without him, I can have a perfectly wonderful time. I'm very content to see friends and be with the kids or do some cooking or sewing that I don't usually have time for, or . . . etc., etc., etc. I can be very happy going out to the lake for a couple of days alone or with the children. He can't enjoy any of that if I'm not right there at his side. I swear, I sometimes think this big-man, powerful number they pull is all just a cover for how dependent they are.

Her husband, a soft-spoken forty-year-old financial analyst, doesn't disagree with her account, only with the interpretation she gives it.

What did I get married for if it's not to have someone to do things with and to share my life? If I have to hang around alone at night while she works or goes out with a friend, or spend vacations alone, why didn't I just stay single? Nothing's much fun without her, so why would I want to do it that way? She calls it dependency, but Christ, I just say it's common sense; most men feel just like I do. Mind you, I'm not saying men don't have dependency needs; sure we do. But this doesn't have anything to do with dependency; it has to do with what a man wants out of a relationship.

Only a few of the men I met had reached a level of self-awareness that enabled them to articulate their understanding of these subtle, and often unconscious, ways in which men are dependent upon women. One of them, a divorced forty-three-year-old college professor, spoke of his feelings with unusual clarity:

I understand now that women have been a stand-in for men's emotional life. I'm not just talking about other men, I mean for me, too. In a thousand ways, my ex-wife, Amy, lived out my emotional life for me. I could count on her to take care of all the things in life that required having feelings and acting on them—even with my own kids. And when she wanted to stop because it got to be too much of a burden, it destroyed us. It was as if she'd abandoned me in her most important function. So

I wound up having an affair with a woman who made me feel alive again. Of course Amy found out, and that did us in. But Jesus, why did it have to take a divorce and three years of living alone and two years of therapy (with which I'm not finished yet) for me to get it; I feel like a fool sometimes. [With a short, ironic laugh] Well, that's what Amy said about me, only I didn't know what the hell she was talking about then.

Why is it that women so often become the "stand-in for men's emotional life"? The problem is born in the same early childhood experience about which I have spoken so much. Connection with another is the very substance of human social life. Yet, as a boy, he had to renounce his earliest bond —a renunciation that meant also that he lost touch with a part of himself, the part that can allow vulnerability, that can experience dependency. Forever after, therefore, he'll search for relationships which offer the promise of healing the wound, of regaining that lost part. But, because the original connection was with a woman, it's usually only with her that it can be re-experienced at all—even if with the kinds of difficulty and ambivalence I have been examining in the pages of this book.

And that, unfortunately, is the ultimate paradox. For, while he hungers to recapture the repressed part of himself, he also remains careful forever about any relationship whose intimacy and intensity are strong enough to recall that archaic bond within which it was first experienced— keeping himself rigidly separate, tightly under emotional control.

This, I believe, is an important clue to understanding why men's friendships with each other usually are so emotionally impoverished. The heart and intensity of a man's need is connected to a woman, not to another man—a need that sometimes seems like his connection with his humanity itself. And this, too, is why men often seem so emotionally dependent in a relationship with a woman while at the same time denying it so insistently. They're not lying; the denial is not just an act. Rather, they're in the grip of a powerful combination of the need and fear—a combination in which sometimes the need for connection ascends, sometimes the fear of another loss, another abandonment, dominates.*

But they long ago learned to armor themselves against both the need and the threat. Internally, the boundaries they developed in childhood protect against incursions from the outside while also shielding them from the threat they fear from the inside—the threat that the old wound will be re-opened, the pain experienced once again. Externally, their social roles aid and abet the denial, helping them to keep these needs invisible from themselves as well as from others. But the needs are there—demanding their due, pushing men to create structures and relationships within which they can be met even if not acknowledged.

A question comes to mind here, a question that asks whether what I have recounted about men and their relationships, about their capacity for intimacy and emotional closeness, applies in other cultures as well.

It's a difficult question. Direct comparisons across national boundaries require that we understand all the societies involved equally well. Talking about concepts like intimacy and dependency across cultures assumes that these are ideas whose meanings are shared—an assumption that's questionable, to say the least. Comparing behavioral differences without knowing what *meaning* a people or a group give to their behavior can lead to conclusions that have little

---

*I am, of course, referring here to heterosexual men. But it's worth considering how this theory could explain male homosexuality without the connotations of pathology that are either explicit or implicit in traditional psychoanalytic explanations. For I am arguing that, whenever women are the primary caregivers of infancy, men will be ambivalent and fearful about relations with them. It would, therefore, seem reasonable that some men would move quite naturally toward relations with men which, while offering the connection they seek, would not stir the early pain and fear so acutely.

relation to reality. For example, some observers may watch men in Latin countries embrace in greeting and take this to be a sign of affection. Yet my own interviews and observations over a period of years with men in Mexico, Spain, and Italy suggest that this is a gesture as ritualized and stylized as a dance—one that has no greater emotional meaning or content than the handshake between American men. Indeed, American men, unfamiliar with the ritual form, will often speak of the discomfort they generate in their encounters in these countries when their own bodies move closer than prescribed, or when they hold the embrace a brief moment more than expected.

Partly because of the difficulties in cross-cultural research, there has been little systematic study and comparison of men's relationships with each other in this society and elsewhere. Such work on the subject as does exist is largely impressionistic—work done from the outside not the inside, therefore, work that offers little beyond what we already know from casual observation. Only one book, Robert Brain's *Friends and Lovers,* published several years ago, gives us anything approaching a depth look at the cross-cultural patterns in men's friendships.* And while his knowledge of the literature is formidable and his style erudite, the data he presents are culled from the accounts of others—largely from ancient cultures or from tribal ones where life is very different from our own.

Such comparisons are limited by the fact that people in different cultures not only live their external lives differently but have different internal lives as well. Sometimes the differences are massive—as would be the case in tribal societies, or in those where polygamy is the norm. Sometimes they're much smaller—as we can see when we look at the differences between our own behaviors and those in other Western countries. There, because central elements in the

*New York: Basic Books, 1976.

organization of our societies are similar, we see similarities. And, because values, norms, and customs differ among us, we also see differences—differences in the emotional expressiveness permitted to men, for example, or in some of the ways in which they relate to each other. The question to be answered, however, is not simply whether men *behave* somewhat differently, but what those differences *mean*— and whether they contradict the theory I have laid out here.

Men in Greece walk down the street arm in arm; in Tunisia they walk hand in hand. Greece and Tunisia—countries where social relations between the sexes range from highly segregated to rigidly tabooed. In such cultural contexts, it's entirely possible that the relationships men form with each other are different in both tone and content from the friendships between men in America. Where friendly relations with women are proscribed, where else would men look for companionship, for comfort, for any of the needs for which people turn to one another?

But this says nothing about the quality of intimacy between these men—nothing about intimacy as I have spoken of it throughout this book, nothing either about whether that kind of intimacy is valued in these societies. Men may hold hands or link arms while still being unable or unwilling, to express their inmost thoughts, frailties, and vulnerabilities. Or the whole issue of intimacy, as we define and value it, may be of no concern to them.

In countries where the norms regulating relations between the sexes are not so different from ours, we find behaviors that are more familiar. The fabled *mateships* of Australia, for example, are, according to Brain, who is himself an Australian, "based on the cooperation between men bound to a common life of hard toil and often futile hopes."* Mateship itself, a product of the early days in the gold mines

Ibid., p. 69.

and the rugged Australian outback, is explained in much the same way as the relationship between wartime buddies—a relationship between men who must depend upon each other for their very survival in a situation where there are no women. In such settings, mates or buddies provide protection, companionship, loyalty, even devotion. But again we come to the question, "What does this say about intimacy as we Americans generally conceive it?" The answer, I think, lies in a distinction not generally recognized—the difference between bonding and intimacy.

Bonding is an emotional connection between two people —a connection that ties them together in important and powerful ways. At the most general level, the shared experience of maleness undoubtedly creates a bond of understanding between men. It's a primitive bond, often dimly understood, one that lives side by side with the more easily observable competitive strain that exists in their relations as well.

I see it quite clearly in my work with men in therapy groups. There's the sense of brotherhood, the defensive banding together against the women in the group, and the competition with each other—whether about who climbs the steep hill to my office more quickly and effortlessly or who's the "best" or most interesting patient. And it was plainly in view also among the men who read this book before publication. Uniformly they were pleased when they read something on these pages that separated them from the majority of men—relieved that they were different, proud that they had undertaken a struggle to change with some success when others could not or would not. At the same time, they were anxious about being different from other men—fearful of what it might indicate about their own maleness, uneasy about feeling so separate, apprehensive about severing a bond they hadn't fully understood until they noticed their own defensive reactions.

More specific bonding—the bonding of mates or buddies

—is given testimony in the stories about men who have laid down their lives for another. But bonding is not intimacy. The distinction can perhaps be seen most clearly in the bonding between parent and infant—a connection that's as profound as any we know in human life. Yet we don't think of that relationship as an intimate one. For intimacy, as we think of it, is possible only between equals—between two people who have both the emotional development and the verbal skills to share their inner life with each other.

It's when we separate bonding from intimacy that we can explain the relationships we sometimes see among American working-class men—relationships which seem at once so intensely connected yet so lacking in verbal expression. In my research, I came across a few such friendships, where all kinds of activities from work to play were shared, where the depth of the bonding was undeniable, but where feelings—whether about one another or about self—were talked about only when tongues were loosened by too much drink. In truth, I came to believe that the nights of drinking together between such men came not so much out of a desire to carouse but, at least in part, out of an inchoate wish to relax some of the constraints that bind them in their human relationships.

To return now to the issue of dependency and the way it makes itself felt in our lives. Even without the cross-cultural complications, the dependence-independence struggle is difficult to comprehend and talk about in its variety of emotional meanings—meanings that often lie far outside consciousness. It becomes especially important, therefore, to be able to hear not only what is said but what is not—to listen for the latent meanings, to decode the metaphors people often use to obscure reality even from themselves, to read the symbolic content of communication that usually tells more than the words they speak.

Partly, as I have already indicated, the idea of the dependent woman and the independent man is sustained by the many barriers the social arrangements of this society place in the way of women's independence and men's dependence. Not only are women economically and socially disadvantaged when compared to men, but social definitions insist that passivity and dependency are the core of femininity while aggressiveness and independence are the central features of masculinity. So widespread is the acceptance of these notions that all the evidence shows that an independent, successful woman is much less likely to have the sustenance and comfort of family life than a dependent, unsuccessful one. The reverse is true for a man. It's the unsuccessful man who is most likely to suffer the same fate, to find himself alone and lonely.

In themselves, these are reasons enough for a woman and a man to collude by playing up her dependency while they play down his. But there's something else as well. Since it's still as someone's daughter, someone's wife, someone's mother that a woman is known and judged in the world, it's still important for her, as well as for a man, to believe that he's the stronger one. Consequently, while a woman today will *speak* easily of wanting to know more of a man's vulnerabilities, to see more of his dependency, when she sees them, her anxieties about what it means for her own status, even for her very definition of self, may rise high enough so that she becomes acutely ambivalent, if not downright hostile.

It doesn't happen all the time, of course. But men see it or sense it often enough to make them resistant to requests to drop their guard. A man's security, after all, depends on having a woman in his life. And on this the evidence is stark: A woman doesn't easily leave a man who provides her with an exalted sense of self. The unfortunate result, however, is that, when we look at both, we are more likely to see stereotypes rather than the human actors who suffer conflict and confusion about their socially prescribed roles, who struggle with the stress of trying to play their parts according to the script.

It's distressingly circular, isn't it? Ideology begets behavior which reinforces ideology, so that it soon seems like an ultimate truth. It's disabling for us and for the lives we try to build together because, despite all our attempts at conformity, we never quite make it. Indeed, the intensity with which we keep trying is itself evidence of the unnaturalness of the effort—something that would seem obvious if our vision were not so constricted by an ideology so insistently proclaimed and so well internalized.

To understand dependency in women more fully, we must free ourselves of our preconceptions if we're to hear what they say about the ways in which their economic dependence creates for them a heightened sense of their emotional dependence. When we do, we hear quite clearly of the many ways their financial position in the family colors their feelings about a marriage, about themselves, about their prospects for living comfortably in the world without their husbands. A thirty-two-year-old woman who works as an assembler in an electronics factory said worriedly:

> I'm scared to think about being alone because how would I support myself and the kids? There's no way I could make enough to do that, and if he didn't live with us, I don't figure I could count on that much from him.

And they talk compellingly about the difference when they become self-supporting. A thirty-seven-year-old mother of two, who recently won promotion into the managerial ranks of the large corporation for which she has worked for the past ten years, put it thus:

> In the last couple of years, for the first time in our marriage, I can support myself; I'm not financially dependent on Fred anymore. And let me tell you, I'll never be there again; I'll

never let it happen again no matter what. Before this, there were times when things were hard between us when I thought, "My God, what'll I do without him?" And it wasn't just emotionally that I meant it. I mean, sure I'm dependent on him emotionally, too—I am, I know that. But the big one was that financial dependence and the awful fear you have with it.

"Are you saying that there's a connection between financial and emotional dependency?" I asked.

> I don't know for sure. Let me think. I know now if I think about what would happen if we split up, it's wonderful to know I would be able to live the same way I'm living now with him. I wouldn't be destitute or on welfare, so it's not so frightening a thought anymore. Then that makes me feel more powerful and not so much like I couldn't live without him. What am I saying? I guess there's a big connection, isn't there?

The connection is both real and powerful, but it's not a simple one. I'm not suggesting that the only thing a woman depends on a man for is his money. Rather, I am arguing that there's a complex interaction between economic and emotional dependency and that, with any adult, a prolonged and profound economic dependency will soon *become* an emotional one as well.

Thus, a financially dependent woman must ultimately experience herself as she did when she was a child—dependent on another for the most basic necessities of life, from a place to sleep to one where she can feel safe and loved. And like a child she will try to bring both her behavior and her feelings into compliance with what the powerful parent expects. Children, we know, don't always manage to do this well—sometimes because they can't violate their inner sense of themselves so completely, sometimes because they're in rebellion against the very dependency that makes them feel it's necessary to do so. So it is with a woman—the ambivalence with which she responds to the emotional dependency wrought by her economic dependency making itself felt in numberless ways within the marriage.

At times she'll seem utterly dependent and needy, unable to manage even simple problems of living by herself. For her, it's not an act; it's what she *feels* at those times—the childlike experience turning her into a child, at least for the moment. Her husband reinforces those feelings when he responds with the same combination of pride and irritation that a parent displayed at some earlier time in her life. On the one hand, he's pleased about this demonstration of her need of him, reassured by it; on the other, he's irritated at her clinging, at her childlike need to bother him with trivial matters.

But, as with all ambivalence, the other side will soon show itself. So, at another time, she'll assert her independence—an assertion that may take an equally childlike form. Thus, a husband may make a perfectly legitimate suggestion for the solution to a problem that yesterday she might have been pleading for, only to have her respond today with a stubborn "You can't tell me what to do."

It's this kind of behavior that makes a woman seem so childlike, so needful and dependent. The cultural insistence on her dependency as a defining characteristic of womanhood comes together with her social role to facilitate the dependent display. The reality, however, is that, as with men, women too must contend with their conflicting desires and needs to be both dependent and independent. For all of us, the child within wants to return to the old symbiotic union—to be held, comforted, nurtured, reassured by that mother once again. And the same child wants also to be able to retreat behind the boundaries of self—to experience the autonomy that's so vitally necessary to affirm identity.

There are differences between us, too, of course. To understand them—and the reasons why the ideology "takes" so well and so uniformly—we look again to the process wherein boys and girls establish the boundaries of self. And again—now in another sphere of living and loving—we see the impact of the fact that a woman is the primary figure of infancy.

Since, for all children, the early identification with mother is so intimately connected with the dependency needs of infancy, rooting that identification out of their inner life means that boys must somehow block those needs out of consciousness as well. That, indeed, may be the only way a dependent child can make such a shift without living in constant terror for life itself. Father, after all, hasn't been in the primary caregiving role. Therefore, there's no evidence to reassure the child that this person with whom he is now expected to make an identification can or will care for those needs.

The self-contained sense of themselves that most men communicate to the rest of the world starts here—at this developmental stage. It's during this period when a small boy seems to change with astonishing swiftness, when right before our eyes he moves from babyhood to boyhood. We watch him prance around showing off what a "big boy" he is. And we ask ourselves, puzzled, "What happened to that cuddly child?" We see him stubbornly refuse to let anyone tie his shoelaces even though he can't quite do it himself. And we wonder, "What goes on in his little head to make this happen so suddenly?" We observe as he swallows his tears when he's hurt rather than let us see his pain. And we question ourselves, "Did I really send messages to engender such stereotypic behavior? I thought I was raising him differently." We feel him twist away from a hug today that only yesterday he sought with such eagerness. And we're saddened at the loss—saddened and uncomprehending.

In these and a hundred other ways, small boys protect their growing independence. Since it seems to happen so suddenly and so universally, we have tended to credit such behavior to some internal male urge to mastery and independence—a part of a boy's nature, we've said, and one of the things that separates them quite clearly from girls. It must be natural, we tell ourselves, if those differences appear in children so young.

Another view of the same facts, however, suggests quite a different conclusion. For it's probable that these behaviors are a small boy's way of coping with the need to make that shift in identification I have been talking about—that they're devices designed to protect him from experiencing dependency needs that he no longer has any assurance will be met. There's anger in his actions, and ambivalence as well. On the one side, the old love is still there. On the other, how can she be entrusted with it anymore when she, at the very least, participated in casting him out of that old safe relationship?

So he withdraws into himself—seeking always to be strong and independent, certain that's the only way to safety. Because they have been pushed so far out of consciousness, the dependency needs remain a constant threat—powerful forces inside him with which he must contend; forces that, if ever acknowledged or experienced, threaten to overwhelm. For, as we have seen, repression and denial cannot erase these needs. They are simply driven underground, where they are less in his control, where they gain power from the very fact of their denial, where the effort to maintain the repression in itself lends them importance they might not otherwise have.

This quashing of dependency needs doesn't happen all at once, of course. It's a process that takes years to complete. And it doesn't work perfectly all the time—partly because the repression is so difficult to maintain, so antithetical to both the nature of the child and his experience until this developmental point. And partly also because there are other experiences, both social and personal, that make themselves felt throughout the years between early childhood and adult-

hood. A boy growing up in a historical moment such as this
one, for example, when the dominant ideologies about masculinity and femininity are in question, may be able to loosen
the knot of repression that bound his father so tightly.

It's out of just such a combination of internal and external factors that some men retain a fair share of what we
have come to think of as *the feminine*. But whatever the
flaws or deficiencies of the developmental process, whatever
the nature of the culture at any given time, so long as women
are the earliest caregivers, the basic outlines of male personality will not change. They may be attenuated by experience
or ameliorated with struggle, but they will remain a more or
less fixed part of the structure of personality—always issues
to be conjured with.

And what about women? For a girl, the continuity of
identification with mother coupled with the clear similarities between them means that she has much less motivation
—either external or internal—to distinguish and separate
self. Separation, therefore, comes much later for her than for
her brother. While that leaves a girl's earliest attachment
intact in a way that a boy's cannot be, it also heightens her
conflict around separation. Since she has no reason to barricade herself against the experience of her dependency, no
reason to retreat in fear from her vulnerability, relationships
seem to hold a promise that connection with another can be
trusted and sustained. But it's also a promise of attachment
that's so powerfully seductive for a woman that it draws her
dangerously close to violating the boundaries of self.

In childhood, a girl handles the threat by turning to father to help her make and maintain the necessary separation. Just as there's no doubt about the ways in which a boy
is different from his mother, there's equal certainty about the
ways in which a girl can distinguish herself from father. Just
as the identity between mother and daughter means that
each tends to treat the other as an extension of self, the differ-

ence between father and daughter is, for her, an affirmation of her separateness, almost a guarantee of it.

It's this difference, and the importance it holds in her separation struggle, that helps to define a girl's sexual orientation. For, in the same way that a mother affirms the maleness of her son, a father affirms the femaleness of his daughter. The playful, seductive, flirtatious relationship they establish becomes the model for her later relations with men —she, the cute, dependent little girl; he, the big-man-hero.

But given the internal psychic structure she has by now developed—her preoccupation with relationships, her ambivalence about separation—the relationship with father develops its own complications. She wants to leave the sticky morass of identity she so often feels with mother and, at the same time, wants and needs to maintain the connection—the reassurance it offers, the comfort, the safety. She looks to father to meet her need for that emotional attachment and connection in the unconscious hope that here, without the identity, she can also find her individuality. But, whatever else the relationship offers, it also turns out to be a rehearsal for the social role she's destined to play. It may, in important ways, affirm her autonomy from mother, connect her with the sense of excitement, achievement, and independence that she sees in the world outside the home. But the message is mixed. For it also encourages the belief that she can live these things vicariously—through a man. That, after all, is what mother does. And, no matter what exists in the relationship between father and daughter, it's mother who is his primary companion, his first love—the one to whom he turns when he leaves the child.

In adulthood, she turns to her husband as she did to her father—to affirm her femaleness, to establish her separateness. It's partly this that propels her into marriage with such urgency—the hope that there, finally, the integrity of self will be protected. The paradox, of course, is that the social

role into which she is then cast too often serves only to infan-
tilize her once again—to ensure that she relives both her
mother's experience and her own earliest years when her
dependent needs and her need for attachment were most
acute.

She becomes dependent in a marriage—financially dependent and emotionally dependent, it's true. But there's
something more that keeps her tied. For some part of what
we have traditionally called a woman's dependency is, in
fact, a deep and primary need for attachment.

But what, we might ask, is the meaning of this distinction? What is the difference between attachment and dependency? Unquestionably, they're difficult to separate. Attachment normally suggests dependency and dependency
usually rests on attachment. Yet they are not the same. It's
perfectly possible—even usual, as the experience of people
in death or divorce so often shows—to maintain an attachment to someone on whom we are no longer dependent for
any of our life supports. In his fine study on divorce, Robert
Weiss shows quite compellingly how attachment persists for
both men and women long after love has faded away and the
possibility of depending upon one another not even a
dream.* Similarly, we can be dependent on someone to
whom attachment is minimal or nonexistent—the wife who
detests her husband but remains in the marriage out of economic dependency, the husband who no longer likes or re-
spects his wife but needs the support and comfort of the
home she provides.

For too long now, it seems to me, we have looked at a
woman's more obvious need for attachment—her clearly expressed hunger for an intimate emotional connection—and,
not understanding it, have equated it with dependency.
Whether lay or professional, we all insist that we're simply

Marital Separation (New York: Basic Books, 1975).

describing what we see—that women plainly are more dependent than men. But our theories circumscribe our vision; the concepts which permit us to "see" some things also disable us from "seeing" others. When it comes to women and dependency, we have been blinded by our culture's ideology about the nature of woman and the theories that grow from that. And women, believing what they have so consistently been told about themselves, repeat the cant. "I couldn't live without him," a woman will say. "I depend on him for everything," another will insist. But what are these things?

Woman after woman stared off into space mystified when asked to explain specifically in what ways they felt dependent on their husbands. It seemed so self-evident; yet it was hard to talk about. "I just need him, that's all," said one forty-year-old woman impatiently after looking perplexed for several moments. "But surely you can say more than that," I insisted. After another long silence, she finally said:

> Boy, this is a hard one. There's something I want to say, but I can't quite get it. Let me see if I can explain it this way. The image that comes to my mind is getting in bed naked and wrapping ourselves in each other—and I don't mean sexually; that's another thing. It's like there's not two of you anymore, just one, because you're so entwined in each other and there's nothing between you. It's something I can't name; there are no words, but I know it's a very old feeling and I don't ever want to live without it.

Is it dependency or attachment that she describes here?

When a woman cries, "I'm nothing without him," she speaks, I believe, not of dependency as we usually think of it, but of that need for attachment—of that sense that she feels incomplete, that a part of herself is torn away without such a connection with another. The fact that she almost always refers to a man when making such statements is, on the one hand, a product of the past when she turned to father to help her separate from mother and to define the boundaries of self more firmly; and, on the other, a response to our social norms and their insistence upon an exclusive heterosexuality.

It's not, I say again, that dependency needs don't exist for a woman, not that her situation in a traditional marriage doesn't call up those early dependent needs and fears when she was dependent on another for life itself. But we hear these words from all kinds of women—those who are financially dependent and those who are not. Every psychotherapist has listened repeatedly to women who are well able to support themselves say, "I can't live without him." Most of us probably have heard them from a friend.

But this says little about dependency. Rather, it's a statement about her need for attachment—her preoccupation with connection that sometimes feels almost as necessary as the very air she breathes. This is the need that underlies her ability for deep and abiding connections with others, while it also consigns her to a painful struggle to maintain the boundaries of self. For this quest for attachment can be so powerfully felt that it can overcome the internal pressure for separation, at least for a while.

This also is the need that motivates the urge to motherhood—not, as classical psychoanalytic theory would have it, the wish to compensate for a penis she doesn't have. And it's this same need for attachment and connection that explains why women so consistently have close and intimate friendships with each other that have little to do with dependency. What makes such friendships possible, however, is the fact that their first attachment and identification were with another woman—connections that were left undisturbed as they moved through the developmental stages of early childhood. Relating to a woman, therefore, is a continuation of that early experience and seems, in some important ways, like relating to self.

Men, too, crave connection with another. But, for them,

the need is not so pervasive and so powerfully felt because it has been blocked from consciousness in ways that are not true for women. In fact, men usually are so defended against acknowledging the depth of their need that it becomes visible only when there's no one to be attached to, or when an existing relationship is disrupted suddenly. Who hasn't watched some "strong," "independent" man fall apart when his wife leaves him unexpectedly? Who hasn't noticed that he's able to put himself back together again only through the ministrations of another woman?

But, felt or not, like children, all adults react in pain and panic at the loss of what was assumed to be a secure relationship; all adults need an attachment to another in order to maintain a balanced sense of emotional well-being. For men, it's independence—or at least the semblance of it—that guarantees attachment; for women, it's dependence. By the time they reach adulthood, therefore, men fear their need to be dependent and women are frightened by their stirrings toward independence. For to violate these social definitions of male independence and female dependence threatens not just psychological separation but outright loneliness—and raises up within us the terror that we might never again be closely attached to another.

This, then, is one of the important functions of the "big-man-hero" role for a man. It's not just a salve to his ego; it's also a way to contain his ancient fear of the powerful mother, the one who, he once believed, abandoned him in his need. So long as the woman in his life remains childlike in her dependence on him, he need never again suffer the wordless terror of his infancy—the dread that came from his experience of mother as unpredictable, unfathomable, inconstant. So long as a woman must rely on him for the very sustenance of life, he can feel in control, safe from the fears of abandonment that lie just below the surface of his consciousness.

These are the fears that undergird the apparent ease with which we accept the social definitions of masculinity and femininity, of dependence and independence. This is why, despite their complaints, despite what they know in some part of themselves, most women join their men in playing out the social charade about dependence and independence. Women act dependent even when, in some important arenas of living, they know they are not. And men hang on to their self-definition as the independent ones even when their inner knowledge tells them something quite different.

Tragically for us all, we not only repeat these social definitions that are so often at odds with our inner experience, we also come to believe them. For behavior rarely is *wholly* unrelated to consciousness. And, for all of us, the power of society is not simply that it can mandate behavior, but that, as psychological beings, we incorporate those mandates and they become our own.

Listen to this couple who have been married for seven years and have one child—a five-year-old daughter. At twenty-nine, the wife is a talented seamstress who probably has the potential to be a designer of fine clothing. In order to be at home with their child for part of the day, she works mornings in a neighborhood dress shop where she does fittings and alterations. The husband is thirty-two, holds a master's degree in city planning and works as a staff researcher for the city in which they live.

> I feel very dependent on Gary in many, many ways. Until recently, I didn't drive so I had to depend on him for everything. I realized after a while that I was avoiding driving because I was afraid of it. I thought if I knew how to drive one day I would just drive off. And then what would I do without him? I don't worry about it so much anymore, I don't exactly know why. I guess I trust myself more now than I used to not to just run away.

There's an old folk saying that urges men to "keep them barefoot and pregnant" if they're to be certain of "keeping them." And words such as this woman speaks give substance to such fears, as do the sharply rising divorce rates whenever and wherever women gain some measure of economic freedom.* But, so long as women are kept "barefoot and pregnant," no one need notice or acknowledge the dependency needs of men—least of all the men themselves.

If she's available to him when and how he wants her to be, he's reassured. He can even encourage her to take more independent action.

> I don't mind her depending on me, I kind of like it. But it got to be a drag to have to take her around everywhere she had to go. She couldn't even go to the supermarket without me to drive her. So now she can drive and that makes her more independent, and I like it.

But when she wants to use her newfound freedom for some pleasures of her own, it's another story.

> Gary *says* he wants me to be more independent, and sometimes I believe him. But it's hard to tell all the time. I work part time—mornings—then I'm with Julie in the afternoon. Well, if once in a while I'm not right here when he gets home, boy ... Or, now that I can drive, I might want to go out with a friend at night—you know, to a show or dinner or something—and he doesn't like that at all. It's okay for me to go to the store without him and things like that, but if it's to have a good time, that's something else.

The husband:

> I guess it's a little unreasonable but I do get pissed when she's not here when I come home, or if she wants to go out with one of her friends. I don't know why she wants to leave me like that. I don't leave her and go out with my friends.

---

*The experience in the Soviet Union and the People's Republic of China, when the reordering of the economy promised to put women into the work force on an equal basis with men, is telling. There, divorce rates soared as women gained economic independence. See, for example, Gail Lapidus, *Women in Soviet Society* (Berkeley: University of California Press, 1978). Here in the United States, the increase in the numbers of women in the work force has seen a parallel increase in the divorce rate as women become able to make choices about marriage that were not available to them before.

The wife:

> He says I shouldn't go out because he doesn't do it. But it's
> different. He doesn't want to go anywhere and I do—not a lot,
> just once in a while. But he's like Julie. She just wants me to
> be there even if she's playing and doesn't really need me. But
> I have to be there, otherwise she's upset or scared or some-
> thing. Same thing with Gary; it's like he needs me to be there.

The husband:

> I really get mad at Lois when she compares me to my daugh-
> ter, like I was a three-year-old. There's such a thing as a
> woman getting too independent, you know.

The wife:

> I keep trying to make him understand that I'm still dependent
> on him. I keep telling him, "Look, I'm not independent; we do
> most everything together; I feel very tied to you; how can you
> say I'm independent?" But then I realize that those aren't the
> things he's talking about; I understand that now. He worries
> because I really am more independent inside myself, and even
> if I try not to let him know that, it shows and he knows.

This is what haunts so many men, what bedevils our
relations with each other—the fear that a woman will become "more independent inside herself," that she'll come not
to need him so much, that she'll be free to leave. But it's not
just a threat in the present to which a man responds so intensely. Instead, it becomes a problem today because it's a
piercing reminder of yesterday—of another time when another woman was free to leave, a time that no longer lives in
conscious memory but whose impact remains a force in his
daily life.

No matter that today many men know differently—that
in their heads they understand that a woman's independence
is at least as likely to enhance a marriage as to threaten it.
The heart has other concerns. No matter either that it's this
very show of independence that once sparked the attraction

for these men. The fear gnaws at them even when they control the behavior it might generate. And the women, understanding their men's fear while, at the same time, suffering their own concerns about their emerging independence, join with their husbands in keeping the battle between them around this issue an undercover one, fought out in symbolic terms rather than real ones.

The current conflict in this twenty-one-year marriage is a vivid illustration. He's a forty-eight-year-old building contractor; she's a forty-four-year-old learning-disabilities specialist. Two of their three children are already out of the family home—the oldest daughter, much to her parents' distress, married at nineteen; the second daughter is away at college. The third child, a son, is a high school student living at home.

During the early years of the marriage, the division of labor in the family was both clear and traditional. He worked hard at building his business, she at raising the children and keeping the house. When the youngest child was in third grade, she went back to school—first for a teaching credential, then for a master's degree in learning disabilities, in which field she has worked very successfully for the last five years. He talked in great detail about the shifts that have taken place in the marriage, his ambivalence showing at every turn in the conversation as he slipped back and forth between pride and complaint. Finally, in the voice of the indulgent but irritated parent, he said:

> She got onto this personal growth kick a couple of years ago and, along with that, decided to change her name. So now instead of Joanie she calls herself Judith. So she's Judith in most places, like where she works and with her friends, but I still call her Joanie. She doesn't mind.

"How do you know she doesn't mind?" I asked. "I just do," he replied. "But how?" I persisted. "I just don't think it bothers her," he reiterated. Unsatisfied still, I pushed him further. "Have you ever asked her?" His voice dropped, giving evidence of his discomfort. "Yeah, I think we talked about it, yeah." But his wife tells another story.

> I was sick and tired of being little Joanie; it didn't fit anymore. I'm a grown-up woman and I wanted a grown-up name—something I picked because it felt right to me; I mean, a name that says who I am. It took a while, but now everybody calls me Judith, even my mother—everybody but Richard, that is.

"And how do you understand his reluctance to make that shift?" I asked. "It's not hard to figure out, is it? He wants Joanie back." "You sound resentful," I ventured. "Darn right I am," she retorted. "Do you talk with him about it?" "What's the point?" she interrupted impatiently. "We both know what's really going on. This whole thing with my name makes him anxious. It's as if he thinks if he acknowledges Judith he'll have to give up everything he liked about Joanie, or everything that made him comfortable anyway." To which her husband gives assent.

> I don't want to exchange Joanie for Judith; that's not who I married. I guess I get a little worried about bringing Judith into the family and finding out I'm living with a stranger. My God, this whole conversation sounds a little crazy. Listen to me talking as if she's two different women.

It's not crazy, however; it's what he feels and fears. Yet there's a paradox here. For this man, like so many others, was attracted to a lively, spirited, independent young woman. "Even her father told me I was marrying a handful, but I didn't realize what he was telling me then." And if he had realized? "I know now I want to rein her in, but the truth is, that independent spirit is what I found so attractive about her in the beginning."

The bind for him is that it's still what he values in her, still what attracts him, still what helps keep his own life feeling vital and interesting. "The whole thing—how I feel, I mean—puzzles me sometimes because she's a damn exciting woman and living with her keeps us all on our toes. I wouldn't want to change that." "What would you want to change?" I asked. "Well, when you ask it just like that, I'm not sure. I just wish she wouldn't be so stubbornly independent. Damnit, why can't she just use both names and be done with it?"

It's an appealing solution, a reassuring one for him. But the issue is not so simply resolved. She does use both names, if only because he refuses to use her new one. And still it poses problems for him.

His difficulty, of course, is not with the name, not even with what he calls her "stubborn independence." Nor is he simply the villain in the piece who wants only to limit his wife's autonomy. Both agree that he has encouraged her life outside the home. She says:

> He's always stood by and supported anything I wanted to do. He may gripe once in a while, but he comes through, not like a lot of men I see around.

They both also know that, in many ways, their relationship is stronger because of her independent life, because she has interests that engage her as vitally as his work engages him. So he says:

> She gets a little too trendy sometimes, stuff she picks up on the job and with her friends, and I could do with a little less change. But I have to admit she's usually right. Look, there are problems with her being out there, sure, but there's a payoff, too, and it's good for us.

But he's ambivalent. Change is difficult—always a source of anxiety even when intellect tries to quiet fears. Until now, he has coped well with her growing independence—according his ambivalence its due, but comfortable enough so that the negative side has not been permitted to dominate. But a change in name seems different, potentially more threatening because it implies that some fundamental shift has gone on inside her—a shift whose meaning cannot yet be known to either of them. And he responds with anxiety, illuminating a reality about his own dependency that was not so easily visible before.

What I have said here, then, is that our early developmental experiences combine with social definitions of feminine and masculine personality to permit women to be more closely in touch with both their attachment and dependency needs than men are. But to assign those needs to woman alone is to continue to participate in the mystification of both men and women—a mystification that serves them and their relations with each other poorly.

Meanwhile, the play, as we know it, goes on. And the issues of attachment and relationship—and their relative importance in the lives of women and men—are nowhere more apparent than in the different balance between love and work we each hold inside us.

(7)

Love, Work, and Identity

*Life is not a spectacle or a feast;
it is a predicament.*

GEORGE SANTAYANA

LOVE AND WORK—these, said Sigmund Freud long ago, are the major arenas of adult life that require resolution if we are to live it satisfactorily. It's still true. Only the problems are different today than they were then, precisely because we are trying out new roles and new rules, because we no longer see these two parts of life as so distinctly separated, because work is no longer only the province of men, love only the domain of women.

"The best you can say about love and work is that they coexist," says a man. "Trying to make it all come together is hard as hell because you're always balancing things," complains his wife. "Competing urgencies," a friend once called them, as she tried to explain the inner sense of a woman who is worker, mother, wife.*

"My best friend and I have this not so funny joke about keeping the home fires smoldering, not burning," wisecracks a woman. "There's never enough time for anything, least of all sex," her husband complains. "I know it's awful, but by

*My thanks to Arlie Hochschild for this felicitous phrase.

nighttime I have no room left for one more demand on my person," explains his wife.

"Competing urgencies"—an evocative phrase whose meaning is immediately clear to all who live in families where the roles of women and men are no longer so firmly fixed. It's a struggle for both of them, but the "urgencies" are weighted differently for a woman and a man, therefore, the priorities are different for each of them as well—as these words, spoken by a forty-two-year-old college professor, show so clearly.

> I break my ass to spend more time with the kids these days, but it's a killer. Carole can step back the hours she puts in at work, but it's hard as hell for me to do that. I've worked damned hard to get where I am and I can't put it in jeopardy. I know I'm missing out with the kids; it's not just because she tells me, I *know* it. But that pull to my work . . . well, it's irresistible in a way. It's not the same for Carole, which makes me wonder sometimes if that's not just the way it is with men and women.

"But what would you be jeopardizing?" I asked. "You already have tenure and a rather impressive reputation in your field."

> Sure, sure. But you have to keep up if you want to stay up there; you can't live on past accomplishments. [Pausing to think for a while, then continuing more slowly] It's not just that old competitive stuff, that's not all. It's something about the work itself. [Throwing his hands up in a gesture of helplessness] I don't know; it's so much a part of me it feels like I'd have to violate my nature. [Laughing] You're the shrink; what do you think; genes or something?

It's a common story even among those men who now talk about wishing it were different, who now seem to understand the deprivation they have suffered in not being more actively involved in raising their children. And why is it that way? At the most manifest level, we see that, despite all the talk abroad about the importance of family life, despite national conferences on the future of the family, neither government nor industry makes any serious move toward the kinds of institutional changes in the work world that are necessary to permit men to take a more active role inside the family. Still, that's not enough to explain why so many men, who believe they want to, have such difficulty in moderating their commitment to work in favor of love.

Over the last several years, I have asked hundreds of people of all ages and from all walks of life to identify themselves for me, to answer the question "Who are you?" Almost invariably, a man will respond by saying what kind of work he does. "I'm a lawyer," "I'm a carpenter," "I'm a writer," "I'm a teacher," "I'm an electrician"—this is the first thing a man will say about himself. Having located himself in the world of work, having said who he is in the social world, he *may* then have something to say about himself in his private world. Only then, if at all, will he speak about being a husband, a father, a son, a lover. So pronounced is this tendency that, even where a husband and wife are actually sharing roles, it's almost always his work that he turns to first when offering a definition of himself.

It's just this that makes unemployment so difficult for a man—this sense that he has lost himself, that he can't say who he is. An unemployed factory worker said haltingly, "When you've got work, you know you're a somebody. It's been a long time since I had regular work, so . . . well, I don't know. I guess you forget who you are after a while, don't you?" And an architect, unable to find work in his chosen profession, replied to my question angrily, "I can't say I'm an architect because I haven't been 'architecting' for a long time. So what the hell am I?"

Both men are husbands, both are fathers. Because their wives work full time and they do not, both men are heavily involved in family-related activities—child care, cooking, cleaning, laundry, even taking the weekly turn at a child's nursery school. Yet not one of these activities is defining of self, not one really counts in the important task of placing oneself in the world, of being able to say confidently, "I am . . ."

For a woman, it's a different story. For her, even a deeply integrated professional commitment doesn't displace family concerns and relationships from the center of her life and thought. No matter what else she may be or do, she's also a wife and a mother—identities that are central to her definition of self, that she'll own as hers whether you meet her in the office, in the market, or in the kitchen. A working doctor answered my questions by saying, "That's easy! I'm a mother, a physician, and a wife—and I juggle all three all the time." And an unemployed lawyer had no trouble in drawing a word picture of herself: "I'm a wife and mother and a sometimes attorney."

We see it over and over again—the different balance between love and work making itself evident in both their private life and their public one, in how they define themselves and how they are given definition in the world outside the family.

Look, for example, at the jacket of a book written by a man. Almost never does it tell us anything about whether he is married, has children, or how many. And the occupation of his wife is surely of scant moment. Yet all those facts usually are part of the biography of a woman author. It seems to most of us like important information about a woman—enabling us to understand something about her as a person, telling us much about how she lives her life. But it's not so about a man. There, the assumption is that those facts of his life will explain little about who he is, how he lives, what engages him. There, we tend to assume we have as much knowledge of him as we need when we know what work he does and where he does it.

"Do we work to live or live to work?"—the question asked by the great German sociologist Max Weber still concerns us today. Love and work—a difficult balance for most of us, but a predictable one. Historically, men have fallen on one side of the scale, women on the other. If we think for a moment about the qualities inherent in the two, we can understand why. Work is rational and cognitive; love is emotional and experiential. Work is mastery, achievement, competition, separateness; love is sensory, feeling, sharing, union. In work, we manipulate the environment, seek to change one thing into another. A blank page becomes a printed one; a pile of wood and a sack of nails are fashioned into the framework for a house. In love, we're concerned with people not with things—with the inner life not with the outer one.

Put that way, it sounds as if we are not just discussing the ways in which love is separate from work, but the ways also in which women and men differ in their orientation to the world. It's not that men see no value in love and the qualities it calls forth or that women see none in work and the attributes that characterize it. But the balance between the two is different for men and for women—a difference that has profound consequences for the ways in which love and work are integrated for each of them, therefore, for their relations inside the family.

We have, for example, all witnessed the chaos that can go on inside a family; most of us have lived with it. And we probably have all observed that mother usually will be at the center of it, father on the periphery. Children get into a fight, and mother mediates. The sound of breaking glass is heard, and mother rushes to see if someone is hurt. And so it goes until, in angry desperation, she calls for his help. "Damnit, can't you hear what's going on?" she screams at him. "What?" he asks as if just coming awake. "Oh, sorry, I wasn't paying attention." "How can you not hear?" she demands uncomprehendingly. "I just didn't," he answers somewhat defensively.

She can't understand his mode. "How can he just sit there without hearing the kids or me or anything?" He's baffled by hers. "Why does she pay attention? Why can't she let them take care of things themselves? Besides," he complains, "she doesn't have to yell. All she has to do is tell me and I'll do it." And she, exasperated almost to tears, replies angrily, "Why do I have to be the one always to see and tell?" Listen to both sides of the story as this couple, married six years with two children, tell it. He's a thirty-three-year-old computer programmer; she's thirty-one, a systems analyst in a bank. The husband:

> I try, I swear I do. But I don't know what she wants half the time. It's like it's never enough.

The wife:

> He tunes out; I just can't believe how he can do that, but he does it. He's not really insensitive, at least I don't think so, but he has this amazing capacity to just stop being there. I mean, he's there, but he's not *there.*

The husband:

> She accuses me of doing some kind of disappearing act, and I'm never sure what she means. I'm sitting right there.

The wife:

> He can be sitting in the same room, but he doesn't know what's going on around him. There's a wall around him that you can't get past. The whole place can be up in arms, I can be like a screaming banshee, and he won't even pick his head up out of the magazine he's reading. Or sometimes it'll finally get to him, so he looks up and says in that quiet voice of his, "Hey, what's the matter?" And I feel like I'm crazy.

The husband:

> I suppose I do have this ability to shut things out. But what's wrong with that? Why do I have to be involved all the time? Maybe all our lives would be easier if she could do a little more of it.

The wife:

> I try sometimes, I really try to do what he does, but it's absolutely impossible to pull it off. It's like there's a radar inside me that always knows what's going on around me all the time, and you can't just switch it off. It's the same thing in the office; I think it's why I'm good at my job, because I know what's going on with people; it's like I keep watch or something.

Another woman, granting her husband's participation in certain of the tasks of housekeeping and parenting, summed up her tale with the common complaint about how she remains responsible for arranging, organizing, planning, administering.

> Keeping it together is my job; if I waited for him to take that kind of responsibility around here, well . . .

Her husband, uncomprehending, wonders why she's so busy all the time, why she makes so much work for herself.

> She doesn't have to do all that stuff; we'd get along just fine without all that perfection. I don't need her fine meal every night and neither do the kids. I don't know why she does all that, but she must have to do it because she won't listen to me.

She does "all that stuff" partly because she's been trained to worry about such things, to make them her concern, to judge herself as wife, mother, woman by how her children grow, whether she cooks a "fine meal." And she does it also because, in many families, it's still the way she's judged by others, still what's expected of her if she's to meet the requirements of her role.

But, even where "keeping it together" is not all her job,

one hears at least some of the same complaints. "I can't tune out, and he has trouble tuning in," says a woman. "She's ever vigilant, especially about what's going on with the kids, and it's not my style," says her husband. For her, it's hard to close off even an innocent squabble, while he can hardly make himself hear a war.

It's not planned behavior for either of them, not something they think about, then do. It just seems to happen automatically, as if it were natural. And, given their lifetime of training—he, to attend to matters outside the home; she, inside—they are, by now, doing what comes naturally. But the difficulty in reversing the patterns—the effort it takes to make relatively small changes—suggests that their early experiences with separation and boundary development are involved here as well. For it's not just his investment in the world outside that's at issue in such conflicts but his very separateness itself—the ways in which he can separate and isolate himself even while being physically present.

There are no rights and wrongs here, no one to blame. His relatively rigid boundaries enable him to shut out the world, to turn himself off; her more permeable ones permit no such easy escape. So she hears; he doesn't. The early constriction of his inner psychic life makes it difficult for him to attend to a variety of emotional demands all at once. Her more expansive inner experience leaves her forever vulnerable to competing relational claims, forever trying to mediate, sort, mend, soothe.

One woman, living in a marriage in which she and her husband have made substantial progress in sharing household and child care, read these words before publication and commented:

> It's really important to say that men don't ever seem to think about the things that preoccupy women—I mean, all the baggage we carry around in our heads. I'm always making lists about birthdays and anniversaries and which friends we

haven't seen lately and all those millions of things that have to do with the kids. I'm always juggling something. Even when I'm not actually doing it, I'm thinking about it and figuring out how to get it done.

Her husband, who knew nothing about his wife's remarks to me, had his own concerns:

One thing you should be sure to write about is that women carry a lot of stuff around that's plain unnecessary. That's a big issue between us. She doesn't complain that I don't do my share, but she's always mad because I don't worry about it like she does. She calls it "baggage" and says it gets very heavy. But why the hell can't she put it down? There's a time and place —but not for my Suzanne. It's always all there for her. I sometimes feel sorry for her because I know she lives with more pressure than I do just because she can't seem to separate things out. But I'll be damned if I want to learn to do it her way, even if I could.

Still they struggle—with each other and with themselves. But it's particularly hard when the issues are so obscure, seem so out of their control. For the arguments are not just over a particular chore but over who takes responsibility for the tone, the temper, and the quality of life inside the home.

For the men, the difficulties are compounded by the fact that the initiative for change usually comes from the woman in the family. It's she who has been more discontented with the roles, who wants to change at least some of the rules, who has a vision, inchoate though it may be, of new ways of being in the family. A man, therefore, even one who believes in the change his wife is asking for, usually has less understanding about what has been wrong and how to correct it than she does, feels the internal pressure to change less keenly, and most likely is more ambivalent about it all. So, for example, a thirty-two-year-old husband, married six years and with two small children, says sighing:

Sometimes I wish I was born forty years earlier; my father and mother had it easier. Mom was there taking care of everything, and he worked without worrying about anything else. She didn't complain because he wasn't doing his share (boy, I get so's I hate that word "share") or he wasn't paying attention to us kids. When we needed a hand taken to us, she'd tell him and he'd do it and make sure we got in line.

"So you sometimes have fantasies about living in a more traditional marriage," I commented. He sat thoughtful for a few minutes, then laughed:

No, not really—well, fantasies maybe, but nothing I really mean. I don't really believe in master-slave relationships. Nobody likes being a servant, no matter how much they try to pretend it isn't happening. And that's what my mother was to my father in a way—like one of those Stepford wives, you know, almost chronically pleasant. But, if you look for it, you see the cracks here and there. No, it's not what I want; I'm proud of her and what she's able to do, and I don't want to change it. It's just hard sometimes.

Because it's "hard sometimes," they dream about another time when life was easier or better in the family. But then they remember the reality of their own childhood homes. The younger women look at their mothers, now at midlife and beyond, who lived their lives according to the old ways, and say, "Not for me."

I don't know who's got it harder anymore. I sometimes look at the women who spend the afternoon in the park with their kids, and I get jealous. Their life seems so leisurely compared to mine. Then I look at my mother and my aunts and see that their lives seem so empty, and I know that didn't work, and I don't ever want to live like that either.

Their husbands look at their fathers, suffering the regrets of a lifetime dedicated to work at the expense of love, and say, "There's got to be another way."

My father did his job just like he was supposed to, and what did he get? No friends, nothing much going for him with his kids, and a heart attack. This experiment we're living is hard as hell, but it's got to be better than how our parents did it, and our kids are going to have a lot better shot at it because they already see possibilities we never even knew about.

The older women, suffering the difficulties of finding an identity at midlife, say to their daughters, "Never again."

I come from the wrong generation, and I hope there'll never be another one like us. We were taught—no, we weren't taught, we were brainwashed into believing that his work was the most important thing. I hated taking care of the kids by myself all the time. I wanted him to be involved. But I didn't even dare ask for it because I thought there was something the matter with me.

Their husbands, pained at the departure of the children they never got to know, warn their sons, "The cost is too high."

I was always so involved in my work. Then as I got older, and especially as the kids were getting older and my boy was getting into some trouble, it began to look different to me. I began to wonder what the hell I was doing with my life. I realized I was missing something then, but it was too late; you can never make up those years.

"It was too late"—words that fill us with fear, that harden our determination never to say them about our own lives. So the balance is changing—perhaps too slowly to suit those with a radical temperament, perhaps too quickly for those on the more conservative side. But, whichever their position, most people agree that there have been significant changes in the last two decades. The magnitude of the change may be uncertain yet, but the breadth with which the ideology, at least, has spread across all classes in the society is undeniable. It's there to be seen in the widespread popularity of the new birthing movements which have given fathers a role in the delivery room. And it's there also in the fact that only the smallest proportion of the hundreds of husbands and wives I have spoken with don't give at least a nod to the importance of bringing fathers more actively into the daily care and nurturance of infants and young children.

Men from all walks of life speak unashamedly now of wanting a more intimate connection with their children than they had with their own fathers. A thirty-year-old floor finisher, who has fathered three children in his ten-year marriage, says with feeling:

> It's going to be different between me and my kids, I'll make sure of that. I could never talk to my father, and my kids are never going to say that about me, I promise. It wasn't just because my father wasn't there physically either; he worked a regular eight-to-five stint, or something like that. It was like he always had something on his mind that was more important than anything I ever had to say to him.

And women speak with equal certainty about the advantages for the whole family when they don't have to do it all alone, as these words from a twenty-nine-year-old woman who works the swing shift at a refinery tell:

> Maybe I'm still more involved with the kids in some ways than Art is, but he's a real parent, not just an ordinary father. So our kids know we both can love them and punish them and take care of them in all kinds of ways. He can cook their meals and wipe their noses just like I can.
>
> I've been working swing for the last year. We worried at first about how it would work, but we're doing fine now. He's home by three-thirty, so he's the one who gets to fix their dinner, and watches over the school work of the older two, and sees they all get to the doctor and the dentist or the Little League, or wherever they have to go.
>
> Before I went back to work, he hardly knew what was going on in the house; now he's a real part of it. And, you know, when the older kids were real little, he didn't have much going on with them, but with the baby, he's real involved with her,

and she's just as leave to want him as me. [The flow of words stopped for a moment as she looked at me somewhat abashed] I know it's kind of funny to say this, but sometimes I don't like that so much, you know. I mean, I feel a little left out. But mostly it's okay.

Actually, the truth is we're both surprised that it's been good for all of us. [Stopping to think] I'm not telling you it's easy now; don't get me wrong. We still have our differences, and working separate shifts is hard—real hard. But—how am I going to tell you—well, it's a lot better than we figured it to be, that's all.

It's better, yes. But it's a delicate balance such couples are trying to maintain—and a difficult one as they struggle both against the obstacles the world places in their path and against their own inner resistances to change.

At the social level, the world in which they both work puts formidable blocks in the path of change inside the family. Indeed, the organization of work itself makes any major reordering of parenting relationships almost impossible for most people.

Half-time work in any but the low-level office jobs women generally hold is very far from an acceptable alternative in any sector of the work world—whether blue-collar, white-collar, or professional. Paternity leave for men is almost nonexistent except in a few relatively enlightened settings, as this man, a high school teacher, found out with difficulty just before the birth of his son.

When I told my principal I wanted to take a six-month leave when Jonathan was born, he said they couldn't guarantee my job. We took it all the way to the school board, but couldn't get anywhere with them either. So that plan went down the tubes; we couldn't afford to risk my being out of a job—especially these days when teaching jobs are so damned scarce.

Even where company policy permits such leave, there often are unspoken, informal rules that let a man know his opportunities for advancement will be at risk if he takes advantage of it. Speaking of his dilemma when his daughter was born two years earlier, an ambitious twenty-nine-year-old man said:

> I work for one of the few companies that allow a guy to take paternity leave—unpaid, of course. So first of all you have to be able to afford it. If you get past that hurdle—and most people can't—you get the distinct message from your superiors that it's not what they're looking for in a guy on the fast track. So, if that's where you want to be, better beware.

And, once there are children, the problems of finding adequate care for them can be debilitating. In families where a woman is either the main support of the household or married to a man whose salary simply will not cover basic family needs, there is no choice. Then, children often are left in situations which also leave parents torn with concern. Where choice exists, the problems often are enough to overwhelm even those most committed to changing the roles and the rules. One woman, married at twenty-eight after having launched her career, told it this way:

> We agreed before we were married that we would share it all. I was already on my way up in the agency. I was in advertising, you know, and about to be a big success; I'd just landed my first account a couple of months before we got married. Whew, who would have thought [her words trailing off] . . . We had it all figured—we'd both work, have our careers, and at home . . . well, we'd both take care of things there, too. We didn't know; God, we were dumb. People tell you, but I swear you don't know, you just think, "Well, that won't happen to me." Christ, we can be so blind and so . . . so . . . arrogant.
>   Well, let me tell you. It's easy, all right, until the kids come. Then watch out. Our biggest problem was child care. It was hard with one kid, but with two it got to be such a constant pain and strain that I finally decided I had no choice but to leave work for the next few years. I thought I'd be able to manage it if I could work half time, but that's no go in advertising. Now I piddle around with some freelance stuff at home —nothing much.

Add to all this the fact that discrimination against women in the workplace means that men consistently earn more than women. So long as that's the case, most women will continue to carry the greater responsibility for raising the children and keeping the household going regardless of anyone's good intentions. Similarly, so long as the work men do and the money earned from it are the central sources of their prestige, status, power—even their identity—fatherhood, for most of them, will remain more a biological and economic role than a loving and nurturing one.

Consequently, in most families, it's still mother who takes leave from work at the arrival of a child, not father; still mother who does the primary parenting, especially in the early stages of infancy. As with household tasks, father's child-care activities still all too often come under the heading of helping mother; he still "babysits" his own children. A thirty-one-year-old mother of two small children drew a graphic word picture of a woman who tries to do it all.

> It's not just working hard that makes me crazed. It's wearing so many different hats each day so that I feel fragmented and ... well, not whole, like there's pieces of me all over the place. He does his share, too, but it's different. He goes off to his job and does whatever he does and then he comes home. He's been to one place and has everything in one basket. And I've gone to twenty places and I'm torn in fifteen different directions.

"Why does it have to be that way?" I asked. "Why can't he be the one to take the children across town to child care, for example?"

> Because we work in different directions, and the child-care place is closer to my work than his.

"Why is that?" I wanted to know.

> I guess we thought the kids should be closer to me so that I should be able to get to them in a hurry if something goes wrong and they need me.

"Why do you need them closer to you? Couldn't he take care of any emergency that might come up?"

> I'm not sure we ever thought about it that way, but anyway, I'm more flexible about my work schedule than he is. Anyhow it's all complicated now because I work at Melissa's child care two mornings a week in exchange for her tuition, otherwise we couldn't afford to send her there. So on those days I'm there from seven-thirty until ten-thirty, then I go to work until four. Then I pick the kids up at their different schools and take them for whatever appointments they have that day—you know, to the doctor or to swimming or whatever. [Sighing wearily] Some days I'm lucky; I can come right home with them, and then I feel practically like I'm having a vacation.

"It certainly sounds like a very tough schedule," I agreed. "You said you and your husband are trying to share these responsibilities, yet you haven't mentioned what he does."

> Well, he doesn't ever do any of this kind of stuff because he never takes any time off work unless he's dying or something. [Throwing her hands up in a gesture that suggests she's caught between resignation and understanding] When I'm not mad at him, I suppose I can understand that. People complain about a woman taking time off because of a sick kid, but they kind of expect it. Nobody expects a man to do it.

There are powerful social forces at work here—forces that not only reinforce the decisions people make, but that are, in some important ways, responsible for them. Whatever the changes in recent years, the message is still: Fathers work, mothers "mother" even when they also work. Fathers and mothers may both worry about a sick child, but father generally goes to work. "I just can't take time off," he says. "People are depending on me." Mother stays home. "I just can't leave," she says. "My child needs me."

In her fine article on the joys and problems of shared parenting, psychologist Diane Ehrensaft points out that, while we're thoroughly familiar with the term *working* *mother,* there's no analog that refers to fathers.* Indeed, the phrase *working father* would strike most of us as redundant. Of course fathers work! Similarly, government statistics tell us how many women in the labor force have children under six years old at home, how many have older children, how many have none. Has anyone ever seen a Bureau of Labor Statistics table that gives matching information about men?

Such indicators of social values are not to be dismissed lightly. Still, there's something more—something that lies in the internal psychological structure of men and women. For, although that psychology is born in and nurtured by the structure of social relations, it ultimately has a life and force of its own. Therefore, despite the dissatisfactions the old ways produce, there are also what psychologists call *secondary gains.* These gains are embedded in the existing system of relationships, and, however neurotic they may sometimes seem to be when viewed from the outside, they offer comfort and solace on the inside. Thus, for example, if illness is the route to the attention of a preoccupied parent, there's a gain for a child in being ill.

So it is with the traditional relations inside the family. Some men now know in their heads that the power, status, and prestige that accrue to them from their activities in the world outside are secondary gains—rewards for what they have given up inside the family, indeed, in all the relationships of personal life. Yet change comes slowly and with great difficulty since those are the compensations they have experienced for so long, the only ones they really understand emotionally. And women, for whom close personal connections are so important, only reluctantly give up their primacy in relation to the children. For, whatever the difficulties of

*For this and many other ideas about the issues that confront couples who are sharing parenting, I am indebted to Diane Ehrensaft's excellent article entitled "When Women and Men Mother," *Socialist Review,* Vol. 10 (1980), pp. 37–73, and to hours of fruitful conversation with her.

mothering a child, there are important gains—the intimate connection, the sure knowledge that, whatever else happens, this bond is a permanent one, the sense of power that comes with knowing she has indelibly marked another's life.

In all these ways, the differences in their internal world come together with the external world to make things difficult for those who are trying to find new ways to live— whether out of ideological commitment or economic necessity—as the struggle of this couple shows.

She's a thirty-two-year-old graduate student in public health; he's a thirty-three-year-old doctor who works at a health-maintenance organization in the Midwest—a choice he made for both personal and professional reasons. At the personal level, such work for a doctor means a steady income and regular working hours—time for family life that a physician in private practice generally doesn't have. At the professional level, it seemed to him then to promise the possibility of practicing preventive medicine with a patient population who could not afford such services in the private sector. The wife explains:

> One of the things we're grappling with right now is whether he should leave his job at the clinic and go into private practice. I know we could use the money, but I'm still adamantly against it, because all it means is that for this more money the kids will get less father.

The husband adds:

> It's a big difference being a private doc as opposed to a clinic one. There's a lot more money in private practice, and we really need it the way things are going these days.

The wife:

> He says it's only the money that makes him talk about private practice, but I don't know that I believe it. He looks at the guys he went to med school with who are in private practice, and something tugs at him; he wants to be that successful, too. He

was a lot smarter in school than most of them, and it bothers him now to compare himself to them and feel like they're more successful.

The husband:

I don't know if it's the prestige that worries me like Sue Ellen says. But I work my ass off and I'm not experiencing the rewards I should, so it feels lousy and I get depressed and wonder why I became a doc anyhow.

The wife:

I know what I want and what I don't want, but I'm kind of torn about it because I worry, "What good will it be if he doesn't do what he has to do? What'll it cost us?" He's trying to change and not be an ordinary man, and he's made a lot of changes, too. But there's that bottom line for a man where they have to feel like a success out there in the world, and if he doesn't . . . well, then what?

The husband:

It's a rotten bind for all of us. I like the predictability of the clinic schedule. I know when I have to be at the hospital overnight, and except for those times, I work a regular work week like everybody else. When we sit down to dinner, I don't have to worry I'll be interrupted with phone calls every fifteen minutes. It lets me be a real part of my kids' life and that's very important to me. As it is, Sue Ellen and I don't get much time together; in private practice . . . forget it. I know all that, but it all costs something, too. But then I guess everything does, doesn't it?

There's no real disagreement between them. They both know what would be best for the children, for their own relationship. And they're both willing to struggle to attain that ideal. But they're torn because they know also that the costs to the marriage are potentially high no matter which course they take.

She knows that she wants and needs his involvement in the family in ways that would not be possible if he were in a private medical practice. And she asserts that forcefully. But she worries about the price to his self-esteem, to his sense of himself—and, therefore, to their relationship—when he compares his success unfavorably to colleagues all around him who still live much more traditional lives.

He worries too—about how he can continue to participate in raising his children if he leaves his present job, about the cost to his marriage if he doesn't earn more money and the financial crunch continues to squeeze them without relief. Ideology to the contrary, this, he feels, is his singular responsibility. If they can't live as comfortably as they would like, he experiences that as his failure, not hers. And, despite his denials, like his wife, he's also aware that a battle is shaping up inside him. He insists it's only money he worries about, but he finds himself thinking too much about the success of others, comparing himself to them too often, adding up degrees of status and prestige, angered because he feels so unrewarded—not just in dollars but in all the rewards of medicine that were surely a part of the fantasies that led him into medical training.

It's not only in professional families that such issues arise. A thirty-three-year-old appliance repair mechanic, married thirteen years with three children, who wants to try it on his own speaks of the same conflicts, both within himself and with his wife:

> We're talking about my going into business, Kerri and me. I've been in the business around here long enough to have a good reputation; people trust me, so I wouldn't have trouble getting work. But I'd have to work a lot harder than I do now—put in longer hours, probably night work, and I'd never get to see Kerri and the kids.

His wife tells her side:

> I don't want him to go into business because whatever money he might make will come out of our hides—me and the kids'.

What good is it if we have more money and we don't have much family life left? [With a sigh] But I worry about him and whether he really needs to do it. I mean, what'll we have to pay if he doesn't get to do what he wants? It's one of those things where you can't win, no matter what you do.

Even before marriage, when love is likely to be felt most intensely, the conflict around love, work, and identity is experienced differently for a man and a woman, the balance between love and work, therefore, weighted differently as well—as is epitomized in this story of a young professional couple who are deeply in love and planning to marry.

They came into my office looking for help in resolving a conflict about where they would live. She has an established career on the West Coast; he has just been offered a job in the East. He started the meeting by saying:

I know Laura's career is as important to her as mine is, and I respect that. Her ability to make that kind of commitment is part of what I value about her.

"Then what's the problem?" I asked. He replied:

It's simple; I have a job offer in Philadelphia that I simply can't turn down, and I love her very much and want her to come with me, of course.

Laura told her side this way.

I feel torn in two by this dilemma. I've never been happier in my life than I have been since I came here. I love my work; my career here is assured—just the kind of work life I dreamed about. I have good friends and a whole support network I can count on. When I think about giving it all up, it's so wrenching I can hardly stand it. But I love Michael, too—very much—and I want to be able to go with him. How do I resolve it?

"Is this the only job Michael can get?" I asked. He answered:

No, but it's the best one. It's the one that will be the most advantageous for the future of my career. It's a career I've dreamed about all my life and worked very hard for. I just don't see how I can pass up an opportunity like this when it comes my way.

"What if Laura can't make this change? Will that make a difference in your plans?" His body tensed, his voice became anxious:

I don't see how it could. I don't have a choice; I have to take this job.

"It seems to me," I said, "that's not quite accurate. If you decide to take the job even if she can't or won't go with you, then you *have* made a choice—perhaps one you regret or one you wish you didn't have to make, but a choice nevertheless. And it's important that both of you be clear about that." Looking surprised, he responded thoughtfully:

I suppose that's true; I hadn't thought about it that way. But it doesn't *feel* like a choice. If I don't take this opportunity, I'll never know what I could have done and how far I could go. I can't pass it up; I can't. I love her desperately, and I need her, but I have to go.

"And what about you, Laura? What does it feel like to hear Michael say he has to go whether you join him or not." She listened to my words with her head in her hands, then, lifting her tear-stained face, she spoke in anguish:

I don't know, I just don't know. I understand how he feels and I know he does have to take the job. I keep telling myself I can stake out a place for myself in Philadelphia just like I've done here.

"Have you asked Michael to take a compromise job here so that you wouldn't have to make this move?"

Of course we've talked about it, but it's not a serious consideration. I know he can't do it without feeling abused and deprived. And what good would that be for our relationship?

"And you? How will you feel if you give up what you have here for him knowing that he couldn't do it for you?"

> That's what I'm trying so hard to decide. But, you know, it makes me very angry with myself that I can't do it with good grace. Then I get angry that I even think that way because it's so typical of what women do. But the truth is I know it would be easier for me to do it than for him. That's just the way it still is, I guess.
>
> Damnit, won't it ever change? Will it always be like this —men doing their damn number and we women doing ours? He says he loves me, and I know he does; I haven't any doubt about his devotion. But, if it interferes with his career plans, he knows what he has to do. And look at me, ready to throw up my life and follow him. Do I love him any more than he loves me? I don't think so. It's only that when a man puts love and work on the scale you know what loses. [Sighing deeply] I sometimes think we're doomed.

There's no denying that things have changed. Many more men than ever before are now genuinely involved in family life, just as many more women are committed to work in ways that are new. And there's no denying either that the conflicts they suffer over how their time is divided, the decisions they make when they must choose, the inner experience about what defines them and what places them in the world are still very much related to their gender. Generally, men still are best at the cognitive, rational mode that work requires, so it's where they turn for validation. Usually, women still are more comfortable in the emotional and experiential mode that interpersonal connections require, so that's where they look for fulfillment. For men, therefore, it's still work that gets their first allegiance, if not in word, then in deed; for women, it's still love.

But the struggle doesn't end there. Certainly, all too often, the difference between what we *want* and what we *do* is a striking one. But the very fact of wanting to change our lives is a step forward—a statement of a new level of consciousness that is also a harbinger of change. For the wanting itself impels us to continue to seek new ways to change our relations with each other and, equally important, new ways to raise our children so that they need not suffer the conflicts as we do.

(8)

Raising the Children Together

MOTHER: *When I put the two on the scale, there's no doubt about where I have to come down. There's anxiety on both sides. If I work full time, I'm anxious about the baby; if I don't, I worry about the future of my career. But I don't really have a choice. I can get another job if I have to; there's only one chance at raising Shana.*

FATHER: *She's a great kid, wonderful. I look at her and go all soft inside. I mean ... wow, I never felt anything like that before. Sure I'd like to be able to spend more time with her and watch her grow. Judy's lucky in a way, she can get to do that. But I can't; I can't take time away from work like she can.*

Such behaviors, and the feelings that underlie them, are to be expected from people who live in a society that continues to foster the belief that mothering is a woman's natural destiny. For, even today, when there's so much ferment about these issues, the cult of motherhood grows, reinforced now by psychological theories about the centrality of the mother-infant bond and a raft of articles and books that attest to its importance in the physical and emotional development of the child.* Fathers may have been brought into more active

---

*For some of the most influential works in the field, see John Bowlby, *Attachment* (New York: Basic Books, 1969), *Separation* (New York: Basic Books, 1973), and *Loss: Sadness and Despair* (New York: Basic Books, 1980); Selma Fraiberg, *Every Child's Birthright: In Defense of Mothering* (New York: Basic Books, 1977); John H. Kennell and Marshall H. Klaus, *Maternal-Infant Bonding* (St. Louis: C. V. Mosby Co., 1976); René A. Spitz, *The First Year of Life* (New York: International Universities Press, 1965). For some recent critical evaluation of the research on bonding, see William Ray Arney, "Maternal-Infant Bonding: The Politics of Falling in Love with Your

involvement in the birth process, but, when it comes to nurturance, it's the mother-infant bond that gets all the attention; father still stands outside the magical circle.

Parenthetically, it's interesting and not irrelevant that at the very moment when women have declared their emancipation in new and forceful ways—when people have begun to ask, "Why is it that, until now, only women have mothered? What is the cost of this social arrangement to the rest of our lives?"—psychological theories about the importance of the mother-infant bond in the development of the child become so widespread. It's significant, too, that these theories are repeated so consistently, with such authority, and with such disregard for any countervailing evidence about the potential for bonding between a father and an infant. Yet that evidence is there for all to see. They may be few in number, but where fathers share primary responsibility for parenting, a father and his infant will show the same evidence of attachment that has, until now, been said to be unique to the mother-infant relationship.

I have myself observed such fathers feeding their young with all the signs of bonding—the eye contact, the reciprocal smiles, the nuzzling and nestling—clearly in view. I have watched toddlers whose fathers have shared "mothering" with their wives make no consistent differentiation when looking for comfort. They will turn one time to one parent, another time to the other—depending, it seems, on the mood of the moment, not on any internal understanding of who can be counted on to succor them. In such families, I have seen small children who suffer a hurt when both parents are in the room sit immobilized for an instant, looking from one to the other, trying to decide to whom to run for comfort. And

Child," *Feminist Studies,* Vol. 6 (1980), pp. 547–570, and Stella Chess and Alexander Thomas, "Infant Bonding: Mystique and Reality," *American Journal of Orthopsychiatry,* Vol. 52 (1982), pp. 213–222.

I have watched and listened as older children make no distinction between mother and father in any number of ways, even in how the parents are addressed, so interchangeable in function do they become.

Yet the evidence is ignored, the studies of these families and the consequences of their novel parenting arrangements not even undertaken. Such oversights should prompt us to wonder whether these new developments in maternal-infant psychology are a product of science or ideology, whether we are in the presence of theory or politics—whether, in fact, they are not part of an unconscious and fearful response to the currents that have swept over us and threaten the existing balance between men and women, between love and work, between family and society.

For it's all these that are at stake when we speak of restructuring the roles in the family, all these that would change if fathers and mothers shared equally in raising the children. Such a vision is not possible, as I have already said, without some profound alteration in the organization of the work world. For many, that presently seems unthinkable. But consider for a moment the many millions who are presently out of work in America. By very conservative government statistics, almost eleven percent of our work force was unemployed in the winter of 1983—a figure that doesn't include millions more who may not have been looking for work in the month of the count because they knew there was none there for them. What if the available work were more broadly and fairly shared by requiring a twenty- or thirty-hour work week instead of the forty-hour week that's presently the standard? Impossible? Visionary? Destructive? Unproductive? All these and more were said when the forty-hour week first was proposed—the work week that we now protect as if it were sacred.

Without doubt, the ideology that surrounds motherhood has a profound effect on how we think about it, how we feel about it, what we do about it. Still, it's neither ideology nor biology, alone or together, that is wholly responsible for the ways in which the rising cult of motherhood grips us. Certainly, behavior and consciousness are adapted to fit ideology. But it all happens with such seeming naturalness because we are, all of us, men and women who have been raised by mothers—because, as a consequence, we develop distinctly different internal psychic structures and, therefore, different ways of defining and maintaining a self. Thus, even women and men who are actively in combat with the ideology find themselves in struggle with their own psychology—counting the gains in their new ways of being, but ever conscious also of the costs, of the conflicts that engage them in both their internal world and the external one.

As I write these words, I'm reminded of a patient—a young woman with two children under four years old. She and her husband are both professionals. She works half-time, he three-fourths time—an arrangement arrived at so that they could share the care and feeding of house and children. One day she sat in my office talking of the positive aspects of sharing parenting—of the ways in which it is important and enriching for both adults and children.

> We balance each other out. In a lot of marriages I see, there's a kind of split—one parent provides more of the love, the other one does more of the teaching and guiding. We don't have that split in our house. Since we're both involved with the kids, we can take turns at each one, depending on who's got what to give at any particular time. And it's brought us a lot closer because it's not just me telling him about what the kids are doing, but we're sharing it.

But, as soon as these words were said, the other side emerged. And she spoke with equal passion and force of her conflicts about working and not spending enough time with the children—telling of her fears about how they would grow and what she thought she might be missing. "What about

your husband?" I asked her. "Does he suffer these conflicts?"
"No," she replied, "there's never an issue for him about
whether he should work or not. I think it's too important a
part of who he is." "And for you?" I prompted.

> It's different. I know I couldn't really be happy not working,
> but it's just not so central to my sense of myself. But being
> "mother," that's something else again. I'm a little embar-
> rassed to say it, but I realize how strong it is when my little
> four-year-old says she's not going to have children when she
> grows up, and I get upset. I actually feel rejected. Part of me
> is pleased that she can even consider options at her age; I
> certainly couldn't when I was a lot older. And I think, "Good,
> you see, it makes a difference how you raise a child; the strug-
> gle is worth it." And another part feels sad, like she's telling
> me she doesn't want to be like me.

I found myself going back to the hour long after she left
—thinking about her words, wondering how to understand
them, trying to make sense of these conflicts I hear about
from women so often. "Why," I kept asking myself, "would
a daughter's words about not having children feel like a re-
jection of self?" I considered the problems so many women
have in separating self from a daughter and thought, "Yes,
that's true, but as an explanation it feels incomplete." I wondered what difference it would make if a woman had a solid
career identity instead of just knowing that she "couldn't
really be happy not working." And I remembered my own
feelings when my grown daughter was doubtful about
whether she would ever have children. "Did I do something
wrong?" I asked myself. "Would she feel this way if I had
been a more traditional mother? Was this her way of telling
me I had failed in that crucial task in my life even as I had
succeeded in my career? Is that the choice a woman must
make? And, if so, is it worth it?"

I talked with a friend and colleague—the mother of two
children who are being brought up in a home where parent-

ing is shared. Unlike my patient, however, she sees her work as central to her definition of self. Only a day or two before we met, she overheard this conversation between the children. Marta, aged ten: "When I grow up I'm not going to have any children because I want to be a ballet dancer, and it's too hard to be a mother and a dancer." Alexander, aged six: "When I grow up, I'm going to be a daddy and stay home and take care of my children. I'll never send them to day care." Their mother's response?

> Of course, I had a pang about Alexander and how he feels about being in day care, but the big thing to me was Marta saying she didn't want children. That was like a repudiation of all I believe in and have worked for, as if she was rejecting my life and my belief in the change that Dan and I have been so committed to.

"Didn't you have some feelings about Alexander wanting to stay home and raise the children?" I asked. She laughed at that:

> No, not at all. I haven't the slightest doubt that he'll develop a work life and a work identity, and that work will be an integral part of his life. I just don't ever worry about that with him. But with Marta . . . The point is that no matter which way she goes—except if she replicates my life and values—I worry about what I've done wrong. Either way, neither of us can win.

It became clear then: A woman who seeks to integrate a work identity with mothering lives with a division inside herself—two selves that stir conflict and leave both mother and daughter in a difficult situation. If the daughter turns to a more traditional life than her mother has led, that's no good. If she chooses one that's even more in the vanguard, that doesn't satisfy either. For both options are felt by the mother to be an implicit statement of her failure; both seem to invalidate not just her struggle for change but her very life itself.

My own experience gives further testimony. When my daughter decided on a professional career, I felt affirmed; when she thought she might never have a child, I felt negated. Now that she has changed her mind about mothering, I feel successful once again—the perfect confirmation of my own life, a daughter who is at once professional and maternal.

A week later I talked with my friend's husband about this conversation between his children. "Yes," he assured me, "I remember that conversation because it really surprised me." "How did you feel about what they said?" I asked. He leaned back, looked at the ceiling for a moment, then said thoughtfully:

> About Marta I had no problem. I could understand why she was saying it; having kids is a strain. But with Alexander my first response was to feel some concern about this day-care program he had been in for three years. And I began to worry about whether he felt like he'd just been dumped in day care, and whether we should have had him at home more, and that kind of thing. So I asked him, and he began to talk about his friends there and the fun he had, and that reassured me and also made me understand that it was more complicated than my immediate worries.

"Once you were reassured, what did you think of then?" I wanted to know.

> Then I guess I was concerned about just what he meant. I mean, I asked him if he meant he was just going to be a daddy or did he want to have a job and go to work outside the house like I do. And he said no, he wanted to be a daddy and stay home.

"How did you feel about that?"

> Well, it's funny. I suppose I had a complicated set of feelings. In a way I don't *really* worry about a work life for my son. It seems clear to me he'll have one just because he'll be a man. Still . . .

"But what would it mean to you if, in fact, he were to make life inside the home and parenting the major commitment in his life?"

[Perplexed] I don't know; it's hard to imagine, isn't it?

"Pamela says it would be a repudiation of her own life if Marta were not to have a child. What about you? Would it feel invalidating to you if either of your children were to renounce parenting?"

No, it wouldn't. I'd be disappointed if Alexander decided never to have children, and I suppose I'd wish he'd change his mind. But it wouldn't invalidate my own life. [Shaking his head in disbelief] Damn, this stuff dies hard. I *would* feel invalidated if he didn't or couldn't make a commitment to doing some kind of work.

For a man, the heart of identity lies in his ability to master, to achieve, to conquer—qualities that are most likely to be given expression in the world of work. Thus, even when he is deeply involved in all aspects of parenting, fathering will most likely be experienced as an addition to life—one of its joys and pleasures, a respite from the pains of the hard world of work in which he lives and must prove himself daily. A father, therefore, may regret a son's decision not to parent a child, he may wish it were otherwise, but it usually isn't experienced as a repudiation of his own life, of some fundamental part of his male self. Let that son renounce the world of work, however, and it can be an enormous source of pain and strain.

But, we might wonder, what about men who feel an almost urgent need to have children in order to assure their immortality, to carry on the line? Such men would surely be disappointed if a son, especially, were not to have a child. But their sorrow would have little to do with the fact that the son had given up the actual parenting of a child, only that he had refused to sire one.

Such differences in values and primary orientation present special complications in families where parenting is being shared. When faced with the choice between parenting responsibilities and career, most men, by far, will still come down on the side of career, most women on the side of parenting. The same couple had this story to tell. The wife:

> When our daughter was a little over a year old, I was offered a good job that would have meant a fifty-mile commute and one that was closer to home but that didn't have the same possibilities for advancement or stimulation. Of course, I took the job that was three blocks from my house because I didn't want to be so far from the baby. A few years later, when our son was about a year old, Dan was offered a job that was ninety miles away from home which, of course, he just couldn't refuse. I think that might have been the worst year of our marriage when he took that job. I was furious with him for a long, long time.

Her husband, who had been listening quietly as she spoke, shifted uncomfortably in his seat, smiled ruefully, and said softly, "It's true, and I couldn't have done it any other way. I *had* to take that job."

This marriage survived the conflict; not all of them do.

Some men make another choice. Then, other issues come to the fore. For in trying to find a new balance between career and fatherhood, they usually must exchange some measure of their ambitions in the work world for more loving and intimate relationships inside the family.

> Sure it costs. Last year I refused a transfer to the main headquarters in the city even though it meant more money and a promotion. But it's a forty-mile commute and the job required some travel, all of which meant that I couldn't be a real father to Lissa and do that job well, too. It's a choice that'll affect my career, no doubt about it, but I wouldn't have made it any other way. When Dorrie and I made the decision to share parenting, we talked about all the "what ifs." I knew what the possibilities were, and they were all part of the considerations.

In return, they gain power and expertise in the sphere of living that had formerly belonged to women alone.

> One of the most ticklish negotiations we had to go through was to establish lines of authority when it came to Lissa. My wife had to learn to stay out, even if she was convinced that "mother knows best"—and she did believe that most of the time, at least at the beginning. It's less now, but it still comes up.

For women who surrender control over their traditional female realm—who join with their men in agreeing that mother doesn't always know best—the rewards from the world outside the home are not so certain, as the words of this thirty-four-year-old woman tell us.

> People make him out to be a hero because he's giving up so much for his family. I don't want to put him down, but it makes me a little mad sometimes. So maybe he'll never be world famous or beat the weekly path to Washington like some of the others do. He still gets plenty of rewards. Just hang around awhile and watch what happens when someone hears he's a professor here. Nobody looks at me like that when they hear where I work or what I do.

She's a social worker, he's a professor at an elite Eastern university. Woman's work and man's work—as separate in the public arena as it has been for so long in the private one. Woman's work and man's work—one always accorded higher status, more power and control than the other, not just in the professional world but throughout the industrial order. Think about it. A file clerk and a longshoreman, a secretary and a salesman, a bank teller and a truck driver— which job has more appeal? Which pays better? These are the differences that are at least partly responsible for a woman's ambivalent oscillation between work and family, between wanting her husband's involvement in running the house and raising the children and her resistance to giving up control—these objective conditions of woman's work that mean there's small return for giving up the supreme control she once had over major areas of family life.

But there also are real differences in the ways women and men parent that create conflicts for them when they try to do it together—differences that are rooted both in their early learning experiences about what it means to be a girl or a boy, a man or a woman, and in the developmental tasks that are required of each of them as they seek to establish the boundaries of self.

The problem is not just who does what for the children —who feeds them, bathes them, drives the carpool, takes the turn at nursery school. The larger questions are: Who always knows what tasks need doing and when they must be done? Who notices when Janey needs new shoes and Billy's hair needs cutting? Who keeps track of when it's time to take the baby to the pediatrician for the next shot, when an older child should see a dentist? Who pores over the child development books and watches every nuance of a child's growth to make sure it matches? Who initiates the discussion about whether it's time to start swimming lessons for this child, music lessons for that one? Who can tell at a glance that a child is coming down with a cold, a fever, an asthma attack? Some fathers can answer, "I do," to some of these questions; most mothers claim all of them.

Of course fathers could learn to pay attention to such details; they do when mothers are nowhere in sight, as any single father will gladly attest. The fact that they don't do it when a woman is around is testimony to two things. First, it tells us how much parenting still is not an internalized part of self for most fathers, even among men who are committed to sharing it equally with their wives. Second, the struggle to make it so is not likely to be fully engaged so long as a mother is in the picture. For she can't forget what he can't remember. And somewhere inside they both know it. Thus, he can rest easy with the assurance that his children's welfare is in good hands, that there's not much chance anything of conse-quence will be neglected. She can get angry and tell herself, "Don't do it, and see what happens." But she usually can't carry it off because the stakes feel too high. Indeed, on the rare occasion when a woman does that, it makes news.

The local TV news broadcasts and the San Francisco *Chronicle* recently featured a story about a mother who went on strike, refusing to clean the house or cook the meals for husband and teenage children until they agreed to help. She wasn't asking much—just that the kids keep their own rooms clean, that all of them take some responsibility around meal-time. But it was a story worthy of page three in the newspa-per, a feature on the six- and eleven-o'clock TV news for several nights, and finally came to national attention when it was picked up by several network daytime talk shows.

At about the same time, the same newspaper ran a page-two story in which one of its reporters wrote eloquently of his feelings when the San Francisco 49ers won the National Football League championship.* "I finally am a man," he wrote. "I've never had one thing in my life—neither my mar-riage nor the birth of my children—that has made me reflect so much on my childhood and early adulthood." In that final game before victory was assured, he reported, "I felt nothing but fear. . . . I was now . . . in the position of ultimate vulnera-bility. I could be deeply hurt . . . it would be a knife across the arteries closest to my heart." And finally, when the game was won, a place in the Super Bowl assured, "A good friend of mine was driving the car as I had the window down and was screaming. . . . I told him to head the car toward Pontiac, Michigan, and that we'd Super Bowl wing it on credit cards. To hell with my wife and kids for two weeks."

An extreme case? Perhaps. He was just talking? Maybe. But imagine a mother even thinking such things, let alone

*San Francisco *Chronicle,* January 11, 1982.

saying them in public print. Times may be changing, but our expectations about mothers and motherhood are slow to give way. So, for example, even on those still relatively rare occasions when a divorced mother willingly gives up custody to a father, neither she nor we are wholly comfortable with the choice. We may understand intellectually, we may even speak words in support of her decision. But inside we wonder, "How could she do it?" And she may have twenty sound reasons for making the decision that way, but guilt usually dogs her inner life and corrodes her peace of mind.

Maternal guilt—something every mother knows about. But there's not even a parallel term in the language for fathers. It's not that fathers never feel guilty, rather that the concept of *paternal guilt* doesn't exist for us. For a man whose fathering is in the more traditional mode, guilt usually will be quite specific: He couldn't make it to the school play; he spoke too harshly last night because he was preoccupied; he didn't take them to the movies as he had promised. When a man shares parenting equally with his wife, he's more apt to share also some part of her inner experience. Then he, too, will monitor his behavior, will worry about what he does and how he does it, will feel responsible if something goes wrong. But, even among those men, I have never seen the corrosive, all-encompassing guilt and fear that's so common in women. As father rather than mother, he isn't saddled with the ideology that has, for so long, burdened women. He hasn't internalized the belief that a child's future rests with him alone, that almost anything he does today will exact some terrible price tomorrow, that an illness may be the result of his neglect, that "neglect" means not being there always and on time.

Whether because of guilt, because of their need for connection, or because of some combination of the two, most women don't *want* to be away all day from a young child, and the need to do so creates conflict for them. But this is a problem that troubles few men. Women speak often and eloquently about how they miss the mothering—the depth and immediacy of the connection that bonds mother and child, the intensity of the interaction between them, the knowledge of being needed, the joy of sharing the world with this wide-eyed little person, the pleasure of teaching and learning together, of watching a young child grow and change.

> I went back to work full time when Jacob was four months old, which was earlier than I wanted to, and I felt kind of trapped into it. I wanted to work, but I also hated to give up that precious time with him. I'm working part-time now because I don't want to give up the pleasure of taking him for a walk in the afternoon. I want to share smelling the flowers with him and watch him learn about the world.

For women, being in this primary position in the life of another is not given up lightly. Thus, several women who live in families where parenting is being shared talked about competing with their husbands for first place in the children's affections. One couple, parents of two children aged three and seven, are typical. The wife:

> I know it sounds terrible, but I can still get very competitive with Mark around the kids. I want him to be important in their lives, but . . . Well, if I could only be sure I was just a little more important. It's awful, isn't it? But I can't help it; it's as if you're not a real mother if you're not *the* one.

Her husband enters the competition with her, but first place isn't the outcome he's after. For him, as for most of the fathers in this position, equality would be the major victory.

> It can get pretty hairy when we begin to compete with each other for the kids' love and attention. I do it when I'm feeling hurt and left out because she's really in the number-one spot. She needs it and I think she makes sure she stays there, and sometimes I get mad so I jump into the fray. But I'm not look-

ing to beat her out really; I'd be content just to be a little more equal.

For a man, whose definition of self resides so prominently in his connection to the world outside the home, the real competition takes place there as well. It's in his work that he needs to feel superior; in the interpersonal realm, he'll settle for less.

For a woman, it's the other way around. Her sense of herself is importantly connected to the world of interpersonal relationships, therefore, that's where she'll compete most intensely. She may have problems with competition at work, may not think it's worth the trouble, may have a well-developed ideological stance in opposition to the competitive nature of the public world to support her lack of primacy there. But let someone try to topple her from supremacy in her private life—not just with her children but in other relationships as well—and we will see the proverbial tiger protecting her turf.

Occasionally there's a family where the father is the more nurturant parent and the children show some greater preference for his attentions. But it's rare. And, when it happens, the self-blame and the sense of inadequacy the woman feels are pervasive. One couple, whose only child just turned four, talked about this issue and the difficulties it causes her. The husband:

> I don't know what to say about my relationship to my daughter; we're very close. It's no problem for me and her, but it's very hard on Alice. [Stopping to think] I mean, she likes it, but it also hurts her very badly when Robbie turns to me all the time. But the truth is, that I really seem to understand her better and I have a lot more patience. [With an angry gesture] Shit, it's a crazy situation, because that's just the problem; that's what Alice can't stand. So she begins to get competitive and angry and . . . [With a helpless look] Christ, it can be a mess —not just between her and the kid, but between us.

The wife:

> I keep telling myself that I'm behaving like a crazy woman,
> but I can't help it. [Looking directly at me] If you have chil-
> dren, then you know. How can a mother feel okay unless she
> can believe she's the most important person in a child's life?
> [Struggling to hold back tears] I know, I know all the rhetoric
> about men and women and mothers and fathers, and I even
> believe most of it. That's why Jeff and I have a marriage that's
> based on the kind of sharing we've been talking about. But it
> doesn't help how I feel when Robin turns to him so consis-
> tently. [Leaning forward tensely] Sure, I know I'm lucky to
> have a man like Jeff who can give so much to a child. [With
> an ironic laugh] Everybody thinks he's wonderful and they
> keep telling me so. But, damnit, what isn't said is that I'm not
> so wonderful. They wouldn't admit that they think that—at
> least not out loud; everybody's too sophisticated for that these
> days. But I'll never believe people aren't thinking it.
>
> [With an impatient shrug] Jeff says, "What difference does
> it make what they think?" [Mockingly] Sure, he can say that,
> but it makes a difference to me. After all, aren't we women all
> supposed to be perfect mothers; and isn't there something
> wrong with us if we're not? How can a woman feel *really* okay
> about herself if she's not doing the mother number just right?
> Tell me, how?
>
> So, sure, I get into a crazy kind of competition with him
> —and with Robin, too. It's nuts. But sometimes I feel like my
> whole self is at stake and I can't help it. When I win, I feel
> wonderful—like, now I know I'm okay; when I don't, well
> . . . it's the pits.

No surprise when we recall that the mystique of motherhood is so firmly entrenched in our consciousness that most
of us still believe it is damaging to a small child to be cared
for by anyone but a mother. A friend, who says her husband
often is better at "mothering" than she is, read these words
before publication and demurred, insisting:

> It's important to say more about this. This is the burden that
> transitional women have to shoulder; it's the psychic residue,
> if you will, that we carry with us. Sure there's guilt and anxi-

ety for all of us who are in the transition generation—men as
well as women—but it's not the kind of guilt that says he
should be daddy and I should be mommy. I celebrate the
change and, for the most part, I'm glad the kids are getting
what they need from Andy when I'm not able to give it to them.
I'm not envious of their relationship; most of the time I'm
enjoying it vicariously. When I feel bad about myself it's only
because I'm not better about doing my side of it.

Of course a man who feels he has failed as a father will
also be pained. But a man can take comfort in his sense of
himself as a worthy and competent person in the external
world; a woman has no such refuge. For just as he must
succeed in the world outside the home in order to affirm his
identity, so she must succeed inside. No matter what her
career successes may be, to fail at motherhood is to have
failed self in some fundamental way.

Parenting is different for a man and a woman—of this
there's little doubt. It's a difference that has not only been
noted in the psychoanalytic literature but celebrated there as
well. Mother is conceived as the connection to the internal
world, father to the external one. Even such an enlightened
neo-Freudian as Erich Fromm makes the distinction without
criticism, simply as a matter of fact. Mother's task, he says,
is to offer the unconditional love that's necessary for the
development of an internal sense of security and self-accept-
ance. Father's role is to provide the kind of conditional love
that inspires the child to self-criticism and achievement in
the external world.*

And, as we have seen repeatedly in this drama of self and
society, the external definitions fit together neatly with the
internal ones. Thus, women consistently point to the fact that
it almost invariably is they, not their husbands, who assume
the larger responsibility for the emotional tasks of parenting
—who have a reading on the emotional temperature in the

*The Art of Loving (New York: Harper/Perennial, 1974).

family. "Once I notice a problem and call it to Paul's attention," says a woman, "he's as concerned about it as I am. But I'm most likely the one who notices it first."

For him, it's the *quality* of attention required that's likely to be the problem—the psychological connectedness that makes for empathy and that fosters the intuitive knowledge of a child's needs, the interpersonal skills necessary for managing the intricacies of his relationship with the children and their relationships with each other. These are the dimensions of parenting that tend to give him trouble, to stir his wife's anxiety, and, therefore, to make him doubt himself, to question his adequacy for the role. Thus, a father of two laments:

> There are times when, no matter how hard I try, I can't get it right. I don't know what they want the way she does. I know, I know—some things I can do as well, maybe better than her. But there are the times when everything goes wrong, and I feel like a clumsy jerk, like I can't win, no matter what. Then she waltzes in from work, looks around, gets the feel of what's going on, and all of a sudden, it's okay.

"Haven't you ever seen that happen in a conventional family, where father walks through the door, takes charge, and the chaos stops in what seems like some magical way?" I asked him.

> Sure, I even tell myself that the one who's not there has that touch sometimes. But it's not just that, and it's not magic, I know that. I also know I'm a damned good parent, and that I can meet the kids emotionally most of the time. I can't deny it, though, if I make it sixty-five percent of the time, she does it ninety-five. She has that ability to be right there all the time that I can't always muster.

There's a truth here—a truth that most people who share parenting most likely would grant, difficult though it might be for them to acknowledge aloud. But there's also another truth. For, in reality, her way isn't all positive and his all negative. Certainly he may often be too distant, too remote, too disconnected from the emotional content of the interaction to serve the best interest of the child. But it's equally certain that she may be too involved, that her "understanding" can be intrusive, leaving a child little privacy, little room for the development of an autonomous self.

Still, there's little doubt that, by virtue of their early developmental experiences, women do have some special sensitivities and capacities for empathy that come with greater difficulty to men. The greater permeability of a woman's ego boundaries means that she is more readily able to connect with another. Her more complex inner psychic life makes it easier to balance competing relational demands. When the needs of children, husband, friends, parents, work all descend at once, a woman is much less likely than a man to throw up her hands in despair. A man watches his wife's performance with wonder as she attends to each in turn. A woman finds herself incredulous at her husband's inability to do the same. She thinks sometimes that he's acting out of malice, out of a stubborn unwillingness to be a fully sharing member of the family, or out of some kind of intransigence she can't quite understand. Whatever her thoughts, the situation makes her more certain than ever that she has some special sensitivities for parenting—a belief that makes the struggle with herself to let go the reins all the more difficult.

On their side, the men have their own problems and their own conflicts. A woman gains some status out of motherhood and how she does it, but what does it get a man to invest an equivalent portion of his time and energy in parenting? In the small circle of his life where such activities are valued, he may be accorded hero status. But to the rest of the world—often including his parents, siblings, and other family members—he may seem a little odd or, worse yet, lazy and unmanly. Furthermore, unlike his wife who, in childhood, dreamed about being a "mommy"—who played at it, practiced it—he never gave it a thought. A thirty-five-year-old father who now is deeply involved in raising his two small children put it this way:

> Being a father wasn't something you thought about. I mean, you knew there was something out there that was called [gesturing with his hands to frame a word that seemed larger than life and not quite a part of it] FATHER, but it was kind of an abstract notion that sort of existed in large type in your head. It was just something that everybody does when they grow up and you knew you'd do it, too, but it wasn't something very personal.

Add to this those early developmental experiences we have examined throughout—the ways in which, as a boy, the development of self and gender identity required the renunciation of his earliest identification with mother, the consequent constriction of his inner psychic life, the rigid and inflexible boundaries that resulted—and it seems clear why his commitment to parenting would be more equivocal than his wife's, and why, also, he would have fewer resources with which to do it as "naturally" as she does.

We have come full circle, it seems. For we're back again at the separation-unity theme. She has problems with separation; he has trouble with unity—problems that make themselves felt in our relations with our children just as they do in our relations with each other. She pulls for connection; he pushes for separateness. She tends to feel shut out; he tends to feel overwhelmed and intruded upon. It's one of the reasons why she turns so eagerly to children—especially when they're very young. With them, a woman finds the connection she yearns for. With them, there are no walls, no barriers, indeed, in the earliest months of life, no boundaries at all. With them, the dream of unity can be realized. Paradoxically, it's the fulfillment of the dream that can be at once so seductive and so oppressive—that can make motherhood so joyous and so burdensome an experience at one and the same time.

These are difficult problems. Until now, the world in which boys and girls have grown has been far less than an ideal breeding ground for the development in either of them of a balanced capacity for dealing with the issues of separation and unity—an imbalance that has enormous implications for every facet of our lives, alone and together. But it doesn't have to be that way. For it wouldn't take some ideal world to resolve the differences between us—only one in which children have two parents to nurture them from the moment of birth. Then, as infants, boys and girls would have two objects of attachment and two figures with whom they would make that early and crucial identification.

For boys, therefore, the connection to a male self would be more direct, defined positively by the primary identification with a male figure rather than negatively by the renunciation of the female, as is presently the case. Under such conditions, we would, I believe, see the disappearance of the kind of obsessive concerns about their masculinity that is now so common in men. And, since boys would not have to relinquish the *only* loved other of their early lives, there would also be no need to develop the rigid defensive barriers against their own vulnerability and dependency that characterize men who have been raised by women alone.

For girls, a primary attachment to and identification with both parents would mean that separation would be less fraught with conflict and confusion in childhood, and the development of a well-bounded and autonomous sense of self less problematic in adulthood. For both women and men, boundaries would be firm where necessary to maintain separation and permeable where unity was the desired result. For both, self and gender would be less rigidly and stereotypically defined and experienced—the artificial distinctions we now hold between masculine and feminine swept away by early childhood experiences that would permit the internalization of the best of both in all of us.

(9)

People in Process

And this gray spirit yearning in desire
To follow knowledge like a sinking star,
Beyond the utmost bound of human thought.
ALFRED, LORD TENNYSON

THE END OF A BOOK is like the curtain coming down after the closing scenes of a play. But, in this case, the play goes on long after the last curtain call has been taken. For, so long as there is life, there is no end; there is only process. And the struggle goes on with a tenacity that is a testimony both to the need for change and to the resilience of the human spirit that underlies the insistence upon it.

Intimacy, companionship, sharing, communication, equality. These qualities we now look for in our relations with each other still elude us too much of the time—not because our intentions are ignoble but because the traditional structure of parenting comes together with the developmental tasks of childhood and the cultural mandates about masculinity and femininity to create differences in the psychological structures of women and men. Inevitably, then, the core of identity is different for each of us and, therefore, our ways of being in relationships—whether with lovers, children, or friends—are dissimilar enough so that we're often at odds, often have trouble understanding each other.

What are we to make of our relationships, then? Dare we hope that the changes we seek can be ours? The answer is not

205

an easy one. For there's reason for hope, and there's ground for caution—hope, because understanding brings with it always the possibility of change; caution, because the wellspring of those things we would change about ourselves and our relationships lie buried deep in our social and psychological structures.

If this book has taught one lesson only, I hope it is this: Society and personality live in a continuing reciprocal relationship with each other. The search for personal change without efforts to change the institutions within which we live and grow will, therefore, be met with only limited reward. And the changes we seek will not be fully ours unless and until we understand where the roots of our problems lie. Indeed, this is what these pages show so vividly—people changing one day and slipping back the next.

Some things are easier to deal with—those that don't touch the structure of personality. The redistribution of household chores and other domestic arrangements, for example, requires only that there are two people of good will, good intention, and a willingness to engage the issue. No small task, it's true. But easy when compared to the other issues of living together which go deeper, are less in our conscious control—how we handle our dependency needs, for example, or how we express our need for both intimacy and distance. For they are determined not just by the commandments of a culture but by the structure of relationships inside the family—by the fact that it was a woman with whom we made our first attachment and identification, by the developmental tasks we faced when we confronted the need to separate from her in order to establish the boundaries of self and gender.

But it doesn't have to be that way. The structure of the family is not born in nature but in human design. What we can do, we can also undo. The idea of two parents who will share parenting equally is not an empty or impossible dream. Indeed, as everything I have written here suggests, if we are to fully achieve the intimacy we hunger for in our relationships, it becomes a matter of utmost urgency.

I am aware that to speak of the psychological sources of our malaise makes some people uneasy. For reasons that are somewhat incomprehensible to me, there are those who equate psychological explanations with biological ones and insist that they lead to pessimism and despair. Yet the reality stands quite apart from the fear. For, as Freud taught long ago, it's only when we have been able to break through to the unconscious forces that so often guide our lives—only when we have brought them into consciousness and, therefore, potentially under our control—that we are able to direct our efforts to the kind of change that's necessary to relieve our suffering, whether individual or social.

This was the fundamental premise of the early days of the women's movement; this is what consciousness-raising was all about. And, in important ways, it worked—not exactly as some of us hoped, not as fully as many of us wished. But those millions of raised consciousnesses were the essential first step. Why, then, do we now retreat in fear and anxiety when we are asked to take the next one, to look directly into the face of the conflicts we still suffer and acknowledge their source?

For me, there is no doubt that—in this as in any other arena of living—knowledge is power. Without it, we live with illusion and, ultimately, with hopelessness and despair. Indeed, it is just this sense of futility about change in our relations with each other that I would hope to remedy. For the defeatism comes not because our knowledge is depressing but because it has been faulty, because we have lived for too long with the false promise that the changes we seek would be easier to come by than they actually have been. Then, when reality settles in upon us, we become angry—angry with ourselves for what we think are our personal inadequacies, angry with the other for their inability to assuage the pain, heal the hurt, and achieve the perfection we had been told could be ours.

But, we might still wonder, where does all this leave those of us who were raised by a woman? And those yet to come whose early lives will not be substantially different from our own? Surely we can't expect that this new knowledge will transform the world we know very quickly. Are we doomed, then, to reenact these same scripts repeatedly, to remain forever intimate strangers?

Important questions to which, unfortunately, there are no simple answers. For it's true that the analysis I have laid out here leads to the conclusion that, given the existing structure of male and female personality, there's a limit to the changes that are possible for both of us. But that just speaks to limits. And we have a long way to go before we reach them. Until we do, there's plenty to be done to ease our relationships—as people who have been engaged in the experiments I have written about will gladly testify. For while some of the basic differences between us may not yet be eradicable, the habitual behaviors that these differences generate certainly are modifiable once we come to understand their source. And, even though some of our internal conflicts may remain, in reshaping our ways of living in the family—with each other and with our children—we also, happily, set the stage for expanding even further the limits of the possible for the generation to come.

It would certainly be more consoling if I could end this book with what would appear to be an easy-to-follow set of prescriptions about what to do and how to do it. But we have had such consolation and, to our distress, have found it brings only momentary relief. And it would also be easier if there were a simple portrait to be drawn, a single "truth" to be told, about how we live together today, what we can expect tomorrow. In reality, the best we can expect to find right now is a complex welter of change and stability—people in process; an age in transition. In this process, there are social constraints that stand in the way of change, and, if we get past those, there are psychological ones that must be met and mastered. And, through it all, there are living, breathing men and women who are trying to break through them both —most of the time meeting with some combination of success and failure.

I was reminded of this web of complexity when, one day not long ago, I found myself leafing through the tenth anniversary issue of *Ms.* magazine—my mind a jumble of thoughts that came and went as quickly as my fingers riffled the pages. "Ten years already . . . The mortality rate for magazines is staggering . . . Amazing that this one lasted . . . A lot's happened in these ten years . . . Can we count on the changes? . . . It's hard to imagine going backwards . . . Not just women, men want a different kind of life, too."

Abruptly, the restless thoughts stopped, my eye caught by letters from women telling their tales of these last ten years . . . A Mormon woman writes of her struggle with the church saying, "I've come a long way, baby! And I love it" . . . Another tells how she became a professional, her husband a househusband . . . One calls her husband "a chauvinist in sheep's clothing"—liberated in word but not in deed . . . Another writes about divorce—what it cost, how she survived . . . A wife speaks of a husband who used to shout his discontent about the need to *help her,* and who, ten years later, participates fully in caring for *his* house and *his* children . . . Another writes that with all the talk about change things remain much the same . . . The divorces, so many divorces —and all the pain . . . The marriages—and all the struggle . . . Page after page of letters—testimony to how much things have changed, to how much they have stayed the same . . . Summed up maybe in this one:

I don't think you want a letter that says: ten years ago my son was born—I did all the child care. Now I also have a three-year-old daughter and—I do all the child care.

Or how about: ten years ago I knew about oppression but thought I could singlehandedly overcome it. Now I know how pervasive it is.

No, I'm sure you'd rather hear triumphs: Last week my husband noticed the strap broken on my daughter's ballet slipper. He got the sewing box out and, to my daughter's delight (to say nothing of mine), he repaired it. The other day I was congratulating my husband on a business deal he had completed. He put his arms around me and told me that I was to be congratulated also because he couldn't have done it without me. How true! But this is the first time I ever remember him acknowledging this. Hmmm, I suppose that is monumental also.

My mind wandered over what I had just read, putting it together with my own experience. I remember the time, several years ago, when friends came to dinner—old friends who had been coming for years. On this night something new happened. The women remained seated throughout the meal; the men rose to clear the table. No words were spoken; we behaved as if nothing unusual had happened. But we all knew.

People in process.

I visit a friend. We sit in the living room chatting; her husband is working in his study. Their (I almost wrote "her") two-year-old awakens from his nap, crying. I move to the edge of my chair, expecting that she'll answer the call of the child. But she sits calmly. "The baby is crying," I say tentatively. "I know; Fred'll get him." Inwardly, I think, "But he's working!" Outwardly, I ask quietly, "Isn't he working?" "Sure, but it's his day for child care. I get interrupted when I work, too."

Another friend calls; there's trouble in the family. Can we have lunch? It's a day set aside to write in a life where such days are all too few. But I go. Driving to meet her, I worry about the time lost, wonder if I couldn't have put this off until evening, fret about whether I'm still lacking that "real" commitment to my work that men seem to have. We meet and talk; it helps her to put the crisis into some perspective she can live with. I feel good—glad I made the choice as I did. For the moment, at least, I know the answer. My "real" commitment is to both—work and people. And I'll always struggle to balance the two.

I spend a little time with a ten-year-old boy who has been raised by both parents from the moment of birth. He's more verbal, more open, more in touch with his emotional side than I have come to expect of boys of that age. I think, "Yes, this is what's possible if fathers have primary responsibility for parenting along with mothers." We can't yet be sure of that, of course. The children raised thus are few; the studies of them fewer still. But the few I know—girls as well as boys —give evidence that the usual personality structure is modified. Later, I speak with the father of my small friend, telling him of my observations, thinking he'll be pleased and proud of his accomplishment. He is. But he also looks at me somewhat worriedly and asks, "But what'll happen to him in the world if he's not tough enough?" The question of a new-age man with an old-age consciousness.

A friend, about fifty, who a few years ago found herself unexpectedly divorced and with no marketable skills, confides to me that she's worried because her twenty-six-year-old daughter remains unmarried. "Maybe it wasn't such a good idea for her to become a lawyer. She's making out so well she doesn't need anybody." I shake my head in amazement. She looks at me and says, "I know, I know! It's crazy for me to say that after what I've been through. Maybe I don't even mean it, who knows. But why the hell do women have to make those choices?"

A man comes to see me professionally because the woman he lives with tells him he's out of touch with his feelings, that she can't continue to live this way. He's pleasant, smiling, charming, helpful. He's a hard-working, responsible, nurturant person—the mainstay of support not just for her but for her child as well. In another age, what else would he need? "Why did you come to a woman therapist?" I ask him. "I've tried a man before, but I don't think he was any better at it than I am." "Do you know what this 'it' is that you're looking for?" I want to know. "Not really," he says, a bit embarrassed, "but I'm finally convinced there's something about being in touch with my feelings and being able to talk about them that I don't know much about. And I want to know."

People in process.

A woman I know talks about how she was determined never to marry a man like her father—a traditional man who leaned toward the autocratic and authoritarian. At twenty-nine she married—a rather soft, gentle man who defers graciously to her more assertive ways. At thirty-nine she's struggling to stay in the marriage and to find a way to respect her husband. "Christ," she moans, "in the reasonable part of myself I know he's what I need and want. But, in that other part that grew up in this world, I keep wanting him to sweep me off my feet—you know what I mean—to be the big man who knows it all."

A man tells me about the reluctance with which he accepts a working wife. "There was a time when it would have been impossible; I would have made her stop. But now I'm trying to understand she needs it. I talk to myself about it. I remind myself there's no reason why it shouldn't be okay; the kids are older; they don't need her here every minute. It's not easy for me; it wasn't how I was brought up. But the world's different now."

A young man I know had, for years, planned a career in politics after completing his education. For the last several years, he has worked at his chosen career and shown every sign of success. Last month he decided, regretfully, to give it up. "Politics and family life don't mix," he says. "I want to be a real father; I don't want my wife raising our children alone."

I give a lecture about some of the issues I have written of here and conclude with words that emphasize the importance of bringing fathers more intimately into the childrearing process from birth onward. Immediately after I finish a woman complains that I have not taken serious account of the needs of children. "Small children need a mother to care for them if they're to grow up to be normal, healthy adults," she insists. Before I can answer fifty hands fly into the air—men and women asking to be heard. A man rebuts her statement with the insistence that he is just as capable of nurturing a child as she. And a woman rises to give the results of a recent Harvard University study which shows that a good day care setting is beneficial in the development of even very young children. Both his statement and hers are greeted with heavy applause.

People in process—women and men trying to change historic ways of being. They make some changes in the way they live—and congratulate themselves. The next day they may wake up depressed, wondering why the inside and the outside don't match. They speak words of change while they do deeds that belie the words they say with such conviction. A man who tells of his support for his wife's efforts to establish a life outside their home complains—jokingly, of course, but publicly—that "things at home aren't like they used to be." And his wife cringes in guilt. Or they do deeds that bespeak change while the language remains wholly at odds with the behavior. "A woman ought to be home with the kids —that's what I believe," growls a man who works swing shift, as he interrupts our interview to pick up his kindergartner because his wife is at the shop where she holds a sales job three mornings a week.

But, even where the language of change far outstrips the reality, the words should not be dismissed lightly. For words —even those not matched by deeds—are not empty of content. They speak to new understandings about the world and the ways we live in it, even to a changing dream. Indeed, they are part of a new ideology, and ideology frames consciousness as a necessary condition for change.

Ideology and reality, however, are in a subtle and sometimes unpredictable interaction. As the new economic realities make themselves felt and women enter the labor force in ever larger numbers, a new consciousness develops that's at odds with the old ideology about the traditional division of roles in the family. Where economic need is the motivator for change—a need that was felt first in the working class and increasingly now in middle-class families as well—it's likely that a change in consciousness will lag behind the changed behaviors. Where the new ideology itself provides the impetus for change—as is more often the case in upper-middle class and professional families—behavioral change will most likely lag behind the new consciousness.

Thus it is that some people will speak words of change without living it, and others will live in changed ways without acknowledging it. For those people whose ideology and behavior are brought more closely together—as in families where serious efforts are being made to put the new roles and new rules in place—there is yet a third alternative. They find themselves doing both—that is, living in changed ways and acknowledging the change while often being discomfited by the conflict their new behaviors stir within them.

It's in these families that we see etched most memorably the power of the psychology that I have examined throughout—a psychology born in the structure of our social relations, it's true, but ultimately emerging with a life and power of its own. And it's in these families also that we see the enormous possibilities for change. For, in their determination to master not only the constraints of their social world but their internal conflicts as well, the adults are forging new ways of being in the world and with each other that bring new levels of satisfaction in their lives together. And, insofar as we can judge from the early evidence, the children in such families are developing new and more balanced internal psychic structures which will permit them to live together in adulthood with considerably more ease than most of us have known.

People in process; an age in transition. Whether we like it or not, there's turmoil ahead as we struggle with ourselves, with our loved ones, with the world outside, to bring into our relationships a better balance of those things that have only recently become so dear to us: *intimacy, companionship, sharing, communication, equality.* For the old ways of being die hard—harder still because the structure of the family remains essentially the same, because mother is still the primary survival figure of infancy most of the time.

Index

Abandonment
  birth of a child and father's fear
    of, 60, 61
  separation experienced as, in
    infancy, 47, 51
  separation-individuation process
    in boys and feelings of, 57
Adolescence, 5–6
Adulthood, as stage of life, 5–7
Agressiveness,
  separation-individuation
  process in boys, 56–57
Approach-avoidance dance, 65
  see also Intimacy
Ariès, Philippe, 5n., 6
Arney, William Ray, 184n.
Attachment
  dependency and, 149–52
  of infants with mother, 50, 56
  see also Bonding
Australia, mateship in, 138–39
Autonomy. See Independence

Bakan, David, 6
Balint, Michael, 45n.
Bergman, Anni, 45n.
Bernard, Jessie, 128n.
Birth-control methods, 4, 5
Birth rate, decline in, 5
Bonding
  father-infant, 184–85
  between men, 139–40
  mother-infant, 41, 184–85
Bowlby, John, 184n.
Brain, Robert, 137, 138

British object relations school,
    45

Change, process of, 206–15
Chess, Stella, 185n.
Child care, 171
  work and, 173–75
Child rearing. See Parenting
Children (childhood), 38–64
  dependency of, 40, 43, 145–48
  ego boundaries of, 54–58
  the erotic and, 102
  expectations about
    gender-appropriate
    behaviors, 38–39
  gender identity of, 54–59
  independence, development of,
    145–46
  internalization process in, 46–50,
    59
  psychological theory of, 44–60
  sense of self of, 53–58, 92
  separation and individuation in,
    51–54, 69–92
  sexual development in, 102–3
  sexuality and separation-unity
    conflict of, 110–12
  see also Infants
China, 154n.
Chodorow, Nancy, 48–49, 92
Class (class differences), 13, 14
Closeness. See Intimacy
Cocks, Jay, 33n.
Comstock, George W., 128n.
Consciousness-raising, 207

Contempt for women, development of, 57
Courtship, intimacy in, 94–95

Defenses, separation-individuation process in boys and development of, 56, 59
Dependency, 140–59
    attachment and, 149–52
    of infants and children, 40, 43, 145–48
    of men, 126–28, 132–36, 141
    of women, 141–44, 149–54
    see also Independence
Developmental psychology, 44–60
    see also Children
Differences between the sexes. See Male-female differences
Dinnerstein, Dorothy, 48–49
Divorce, 153–54

Earning power, male-female differences in, 32–33, 174
Economic dependence of women, 126, 142–43, 149
Ego boundaries, 54–58, 92–94
Ehrensaft, Diane, 175–76
Ehrhardt, Anke A., 55n.
Emotional dependence
    of men on women, 126–28, 132–36, 141
    of women, 143–44, 149
Emotions (feelings)
    as female domain, 71–74
    friendships and, 129–32
    logic of, 74
    male-female differences in awareness and expression of, 69–77, 82–83
    repression or denial of, by men, 71, 82–83
    verbal expression of, 75–78, 82, 101–2
Empathy, development of, in women, 58–59

Engel, Elliot, 131n.
Erotic, the, 102
Exclusivity (exclusive relationships), men's need for, 60–62

Fairbairn, W. R. D., 45
Father
    bonding between infant and, 185–86
    gender identification of boys and, 56
    girls' internalization of, 59
    more intimate connection with their children desired by, 171–72
    paternity leave, 172–73
    resentment at the birth of first child, 59–62
    separation process in girls and, 147–48
    sexual orientation of daughter and, 148
Fathering, 42, 62
    guilt and, 196
    see also Parenting
Feelings. See Emotions
Female sexuality
    boundary issues in, 111–12
    development of, 102–3
    lesbians, 105
    mixed feelings of power, vulnerability, and pleasure, 109–10
    need to be held and hugged, 114–17
    orgasm, 114–16
    relational context of, 113–14
    repression of first erotic attachment, 110–11
    very sexually active women, 113–15
Femininity, 13
    see also Gender identity; Lesbians; Sexuality

Financial dependency. *See*
   Economic dependence
Fraiberg, Selma, 184*n.*
Freud, Sigmund, 44, 66, 160
Friendships
   intimacy in, 94
   between men, 129–32, 135, 136*n.*,
     137–40
   between men and women, 129–30
   between women, 103, 105, 129–30,
     151
Fromm, Erich, 200

Gender identity, 54–59
Greece, 138
Guilt, maternal versus paternal,
   196

Happiness, 7
Helsing, Knud J., 128*n.*
Hochschild, Arlie, 160*n.*
Homosexuality, male, 104–5, 136*n.*
   boundary problems in, 112–13
Housework (housekeeping), 35, 127,
   166, 171

Identification, in infancy, 50, 56,
   59, 146–48
Identity
   gender, 54–59
   work and, 162–63, 191
Impotence, 116
Incest taboo, 102
Income, male-female differences
   in, 32–33, 174
Independence, 26, 120–28
   associated with strength, 121,
     122
   of boys, 145–46
   definitions of, 120–21
   remarriage and, 122–25
   of women, 154–59
   see also Dependency
Individuation. *See* Separation and
   individuation, period of

Infants
   bonding between father and,
     185–86
   bonding between mother and, 41,
     184–85
   dependency of, 40, 43
   identification in, 50, 56, 59, 146,
     147
   internalized mother of, 47, 48
   separation experienced as
     abandonment by, 47, 51
   sexuality and, 102
   women as primary caretakers of,
     42–44, 49–50
Intellect. *See* Mind
Internalization, 46–50, 59
Intimacy (intimate relationships),
   65–97
   acceptance of the "real me" and,
     68–69
   ambivalence of women toward,
     84–88, 92–97
   bonding distinguished from, 140
   boundaries of the self and, 92–94
   in courtship, 94–95
   definitions of, 67
   as everyday experience, 67–68
   in friendships, 94
   between men, 138–40
   nurturance and, 88–91
   as putting away the masks, 68–69
   sexuality and, 101–2
   as shared inner life, 79–80
   withdrawal of men from, 81–83
   words (talking) and, 75–78, 82

Jacoby, Russell, 4
Jung, Carl, 72–73

Kennell, John H., 184*n.*
Klaus, Marshall H., 184*n.*
Klein, Melanie, 45

Lapidus, Gail, 154*n.*
Lesbians, 105, 111, 112

Living-together relationships,
123
Longevity, increase in, 5
Love, balance between work and,
160–64, 169–70, 180

Mahler, Margaret S., 45*n.*, 49
Male-female differences, 12–13
in awareness and expression of
feelings, 69–77, 82–83
in earning power, 32–33, 174
exclusive relationships, men's
need for, 60–62
in inner psychic life, 62–63, 69,
167
in intimacy. *See* Intimacy
in negotiation of relationships,
62–63
in nurturance, 88–91
see also Gender identity; Sex-role
stereotypes; *and specific
topics*
Male sexuality
development of, 102
emotional expression through
sex, 110
as "essence of manhood," 107–8
fears and threatening emotions
associated with, 108–10
homosexuality, 104, 136*n.*, 112–13
impotence, 116
separation between the
emotional and the sexual,
105–7, 110, 113
see also Sexuality
Mann, Thomas, 75
Marriage
dependence of women in, 149,
151
old idea of, 1–3
separation and unity issues in,
52–53
Masculinity, 13
see also Gender identity
Masturbation, 103, 104

Mateship, 138–39
Mind (intellect), as male domain,
72–73
Money, John, 55
Motherhood
cult (ideology) of, 184–87, 199–200
need for attachment and urge to,
151
Mother-infant bond, 41, 184–85
Mothering, 42, 62
guilt and, 196
see also Parenting
Mother(s)
attachment of infant to, 50, 56
as emotional managers in the
family, 63, 200–1
gender identity of children and,
54–59
identification of infant with, 56,
59, 146–48
internalization of, 46–50, 59
as primary caregivers of infancy,
42–44, 49–50
repression of identification with,
of boys, 55–57, 59, 60, 63
separation of child from, 51–54,
69, 92
see also Motherhood;
Mother-infant bond;
Mothering;
Separation-individuation,
period of

Newsweek, 131
Nurturance
intimacy and, 88–91
sexual, 91

Object relations, 45, 49
see also Internalization
Orgasm, 114–17

Parenting
competition between mother and
father in, 197–98

Parenting *(cont.)*
  developmental experiences of
    men and women and, 202–3
  guilt and, 196
  quality of attention required by,
    201
  separation-unity conflict and,
    203–4
  shared, 172–77, 185–98, 206–7
  special sensitivities of women
    for, 202
  work and reordering
    relationships of, 172–77,
    186–93
  see also Fathering; Mothering
Paternity leave, 172–73
Penis, as an organ of identity,
    57–58
Pine, Fred, 45*n.*
Pre-oedipal period, 45
Process, people in, 209–15
Psychoanalytic theory, 44, 45

Rationality, as male domain,
    71–74
Remarriage, 122–25
Rubin, Lillian Breslow, 13*n.*, 34*n.*,
    124*n.*

Schlafly, Phyllis, 37
Secondary gains from traditional
    relationships, 176–77
Self
  boundaries of, 54–58, 92–94
  development of a sense of, 53–58,
    92
Self-sufficiency. *See* Independence
Separation
  as abandonment, infants'
    experience of, 47, 51
  in adulthood, 52
  intimacy and issue of, 92–96
Separation and individuation,
    period of, 51–54, 69, 92, 147–48,
    203–204

Separation-unity conflict
  parenting and, 203–4
  sexuality and, 110–12
Sex differences. *See* Male-female
  differences
Sex-role stereotypes, 39
  supporting the family and,
    22–27
Sexuality, 98–119
  children and development of,
    102–3
  emotional component of, 101–7
  erotic component of, 102–4
  masturbation, 103, 104
  need to be held and hugged,
    114–17
  orgasm, 114–17
  separation-unity conflict of
    childhood and, 110–12
  social attitudes about, 100–2
  see also Female sexuality;
    Homosexuality, male;
    Lesbians; Male sexuality
Sexual nurturance, 91
Shorter, Edward, 41
Social class, 13, 14
Social factors, 10–11, 206
  changes in family life and,
    4–5
  shared parenting and, 175–76
Socialization, 39
Soviet Union, 154*n.*
Spitz, René A., 184*n.*
Stoller, Robert J., 55*n.*
Stone, Lawrence, 41
Strength, independence associated
  with, 121, 122
Strober, Myra H., 33*n.*
Struggle, life as, 7–9
Supporting the family,
  responsibility for, 22–27
Susser, Mervyn, 128*n.*
Symbiotic bond, 50, 52
  between lesbians, 111, 112
Szklo, Moyses, 128*n.*

Talking, intimacy and, 75–78, 82
Therapy, monitoring feelings in,
    69–70
Thomas, Alexander, 185*n.*
Triangular configuration of
    women's internal life, 59, 62
Transition, process of, 209–15
Tunisia, 138

Unemployment, 162
Unity, separation and, 51–53,
    203–204

Vulnerability, men's fear of
    showing, 70

Wages, male-female differences in,
    32–33, 174
Weber, Max, 164
Weiss, Robert, 149

Winnicott, D. W., 45*n.*, 51
Withdrawal of men from intimacy,
    81–83
Words, intimacy and, 75–78, 82
Work, 169–82
    balance between love and,
        160–64, 169–170, 180
    child care and, 173–75
    as definition of oneself, 162–63
    identity and, 191
    reordering of parenting
        relationships and, 172–77,
        186–93
    see also Supporting the family,
        responsibility for
Working-class families, 34–35
Working mothers, 33–35, 175–76
    see also Supporting the family,
        responsibility for; Work